Praise for Donna Minkowitz's *Ferocious Romance*

"Utterly entrancing ... Donna Minkowitz introspects herself bare, and then with a breathtakingly fluent language of alternating waggery and sincerity, tells how she incorporated her doubts and certainties into that rarest thing: an authentic self. In this brilliantly funny, wise, joyful book, she achieves the compassion and depth that both the gay and right-wing movements profess to want, and fail to achieve: and she does so with a gentle lightness and forthright courage by which even a die-hard partisan would have to be swayed."
— Andrew Solomon, author, *Far from the Tree*

"An original, energetic and witty book.... Reveal[s] something meaty about real people with grace, humor, and intelligence."
— Mary Gaitskill, the *New York Observer*

"Donna Minkowitz's writing is a tonic."
— Naomi Wolf

"Original and provocative."
— Susan Faludi

"Infuriating, insightful, hilarious.... Deserves a wide readership among activists and right-wingers alike."
—Patrick Califia, author, *Public Sex*

GROWING UP GOLEM

HOW I SURVIVED MY MOTHER, BROOKLYN
AND SOME REALLY BAD DATES

DONNA MINKOWITZ

For Steven Fetherhuff,
who taught me literally how to stand up straight,
and Irving Kizner, who taught me how to do it figuratively

Everything in this book is true, except the parts concerning magic and time travel.

Most names and some identifying details have been changed.

I may know a very little about Gnosticism, but I am no scholar of it. And alas, I am most certainly no expert on the Kabbalah, alchemy, or Jewish religion. I apologize for any inadvertent errors.

"The Human-stories of the elves are doubtless full of the Escape from Deathlessness."

— J.R.R. Tolkien, "On Fairy-Stories"

CHAPTER ONE

My mother loved to make things. One day, when I was thirty-two, my mother created a giant, half-life-size doll that looked just like me. (This is absolutely true.) It had yarn hair the same color and kink as mine, and real corduroy pants just like the ones I wear. My mother called it the Dyke Donna doll. (Mom was very pro-gay and lesbian, so she always felt very happy using words like "dyke.") The doll wore a stripey red shirt like a circus performer, along with real, removable, bright red booties made of felt, and extravagantly long curling eyelashes that my mother drew in by hand, quite lovingly. It had big red apple blush-marks on its cheeks, like Pinocchio as I have always seen him drawn. It stood a discomfiting three feet tall (I myself am only five feet two). My mother gave it to me as her gift, to keep in my tiny apartment. I had to keep it under my bed because I couldn't bear to see it sitting in my chair. But I felt like I was hiding a child away there, without food or anyone to talk to.

Starting in her early 20s, my mother had made a whole series of dolls and wooden soldiers and little straw figurines and puppets, and I believe that one of them was me. A few years after the Dyke Donna doll appeared, my arms broke. (This, also, is true.) I don't mean that my *arm bones* broke— I've never had a broken bone—but that my arms' capacity as limbs, their functionality and coherence, suddenly ended.

It was as though my hands had simply stopped being

hands. They began to hurt so badly that I didn't want to do anything with them, because that only made them hurt more.

I was a writer. I am a writer. And it hurt to write, just like anything else people do with their hands, which basically destroyed me. But forget about "me" and my twee artiness and ridiculous ego— please just forget, reader!—because what I'm really afraid of telling you about, really, really afraid, is the pain. The pain from that time, when it began, thirteen years ago, still seems magical to me, as though it could happen again at any moment. Just by thinking about it.

As I write—with voice dictation software, the only way I can from now on—it's almost happening again. I couldn't lie about how scared I am of this, it would make me vomit. My hands start to feel as though they're rolling in rocks...

A mysterious tension in my arms, like a salt battery beginning to work.

It hurt, that March it started, in my upper back, shoulders, forearms, wrists, hands and neck. Sometimes even my head, by means of a process I couldn't begin to comprehend. Sometimes it burned, as though hot metal were in my shoulders. The hands were the worst, with knives sticking in the palms. I had a sensation of spears through the wrists. Had I suddenly become a Christian martyr? But the pain wasn't even agreeably sexual, as it might have been if I'd turned into Saint Sebastian. It was impossible to aestheticize it without—begging your pardon— throwing up. The backs of my hands felt as though they were being repeatedly forced to move through a basin full of tiny, crushed metal balls, like in some Star Trek punishment from a newly-contacted planet.

This happened suddenly. I was having sex with a married woman—well, a woman married to another woman, and occupied as well with two small children—when my attack occurred.

All right, I wasn't *in the very act of* having sex with her when it happened—God does not work in such linear-narrative ways. And, if you're wondering *why* my attack occurred, why God caused it, they weren't precisely, absolutely married—in point of fact, they had an open relationship. But almost—I was almost in the very moment of having sex with her, and they were very nearly married, except that they had sex with other people. I don't even believe in a punitive God. I don't even believe that "things happen for a reason"!

But it happened. And I couldn't tell why. It was around Purim, and everything in my life had stopped making sense. I went to a lecture at Makor, a conventional yet profound and funky Jewish center—I live in New York City, where we have such things—called "Stop Making Sense—Purim's Radical Message."

It turned out to be a sort of class, led by a strangely left-leaning Orthodox rabbi. I remember that I couldn't raise my hands in the class because it hurt. The pain had begun just that week. I was trying not to worry about it too much, although I had a peculiar presentiment that my life had changed. I asked the young guy sitting next me to raise his hand for me when I wanted to talk. I flirted with a nice woman in the next row who turned out to be from my neighborhood, beautiful Park Slope, Brooklyn. The rabbi was talking about how every Jew was required to get so drunk on Purim that they couldn't tell Mordecai, the one who saved us all in this story, from Haman, the one who tried to exterminate us.

Now, Purim has always been my favorite Jewish holiday because it is a holiday about catastrophe—only the Jews would be crazy and brave enough to have a holiday about catastrophe, tragedy, trauma itself. On Purim you were supposed to dress in costume, get drunk off your ass—the Orthodox guy was only stating basic Jewish law to us—and act psychotic, because you were so freaked out that some people had long ago tried to kill you.

That morning, I'd decided to break up with Gemma, the woman with the frolicsome partner and the kids, who had said to me yearningly the first time she kissed me, "I want to give

3

you pain!" The yearning quality had surprised me, moved me. Gemma's voice was blonde, like unfiltered honey, and it had a crazy warmth to it. I'd decided to break up with Gemma, but to have one last date, one final cataclysmic ending with her, before we did.

But I was sad—oh, reader, even though I was the one doing the breaking up, even though Gemma was a thoroughly modern girl who never got emotional about women and I was trying hard to be one, too, someplace so far away I couldn't taste it I was very, very sad.

My mother, who was pretty cataclysmic or catastrophic in her own right, had been about to die for decades, and was finally, anticlimactically doing it. ("Your mom's dying?" my friend Harry asked when I told him, a year and a half before she actually did, as it happened. He rolled his eyes at me theatrically. "Um, you told me that three years ago!") My mother had begun telling us she was dying around 1972. An operation that she'd had for cancer of the larynx, when I was seven, had been a great success, although it left her with a large, permanent opening in her neck that she referred to conversationally as "my hole." She breathed through it. It looked a little bit bloody, but she would cover it with baby-napkin bibs or flowered scarves.

The hole worked pretty well, but she said it left her vulnerable to breathing a lot of "particulate matter," which causes asthma and emphysema. And so my mother had begun planning her funeral when I was still at PS 197, choosing a guest list and announcing what works of literature should be read aloud (she particularly wanted me to read a long Kurt Vonnegut excerpt that began, "God made mud."). She wanted classy food to be served, like dark chocolates and champagne. Later, as we entered a new millennium, my sister Josie and I had a "dying party" with her one evening, when she was certain she would go that night. I brought her favorite foods, wine spritzers and a hot fudge sundae, and we sang to her. The dying had started when I was eight; I was now pushing forty.

4

In addition to my mother's being finally (maybe) ready to pass, other anticlimaxes had been bursting out all over my life. I had just broken up what I'd considered a marriage, to a gay man by whom I not only never got *shtupped*, but usually didn't get my phone calls returned. Perhaps this was a series of crumbly anticlimaxes, because just before *that*, Edna, my therapist of twelve years, had suddenly dumped *Qme*. She said she'd just realized that our therapy wasn't working.

And then my arms suddenly fell apart, too. They had lost their ability to do much more than flap.

My first book had come out—to poor sales, naturally, although my editor had said the book would make me "the next Susan Faludi"—just before Edna ditched me. Before that I'd left the *Village Voice*, my sole and tightly-gripped foothold in the writing world, because they had promised to make me an official, salaried staff writer and had gone back on it. (This was the good *Village Voice* of years ago, reader—pardon me for saying so!—not the current one.) Me, I had slipped into the *Voice* at the age of twenty-two and snuck, wormed, even stolen my way into writing for them. Why else would the paper I believed in more than any other publication in the country publish me? I wasn't a real person, and I knew it. I have always been a makeshift, artificial person, like a scary marionette or a ventriloquist's dummy, and I have always known I would be found out someday and punished for my evil dissimulation.

I have known I was a magical being, hand-crafted rather than born, from my earliest days. I'm not sure when I first found out, but it goes back at least to the time my mother, when I was four, began telling me and my sisters that she herself could perform magic, could make us do whatever she wanted, like puppets.

She also could tell whatever we were thinking.

My great-grandmother, a Romanian Jew, knew the "gypsy signs" that could tell you what was about to happen—say, by looking at a frozen tree or a dead animal found by the river, and other potent pagan peasant magics that she taught my mother. My great-grandfather, a Jew from Austria, taught my mom wild Hasidic magics that he'd quietly mined from Kabbalah and Martin Buber.

My mother was an extraordinarily— at times revoltingly—creative person, so it was no great stretch to believe she had shaped me like a golem or a living toy, embedded with unnatural life-force like a hobgoblin conjured from a stale half-brownie and a brittle, faded page or two of Keats or Shelley.

Have you ever heard of golems, the source of my mother's first, simple recipe, reader? Oh *goyische* or unmystical, read here: golems are artificial persons that learned sixteenth century rabbis made out of wet clay, to do everything their makers told them to, and to attack the people who were lynching Jews all over Eastern Europe. They were all eventually snuffed out by their creators, except me. I survived my mother.

My mother added a few special items to the clay that she'd begun with, no doubt because she wanted to be fancy. I had polyurethane in me, I could tell, and psychically potent bits of tin and panty and old paper that she'd discovered at garage sales and a vintage store. Some paint-encrusted nails, chipped tiny screws. Dirty rags that she did not wash, so that their previous owners' human perfumes might waft through me and provide a power of their own. A few crumbs of wet muffin. I have tried for years to find out exactly what she assembled on her kitchen floor before she said that ridiculous mix of Hebrew and Coptic words. Even now, almost everything I've said is guesswork. (Did she cut her fingernails at least to make some protein and collagen to go into me?)

It was the 1960s, generally too early for cybernetics, but my mother was a brilliant woman and well aware of Alan Turing's theories, and she may have put an early self-aware chip in me. (If so, the first and second laws of robotics would require that it did not displace the pagan magics constituting me, but added to them.)

Golems (and robots) are but two species of our kind, of course. Many clumps of mud on several continents have been over-stimulated with unnatural spirit this way, by persons of power like my mother, for millennia. Certain rocks and springs have been galvanized (for eons) with a painful awareness, and there are young girls (and boys) imprisoned in eleven-inch Barbie dolls, living spirits imprisoned in bottle caps, baseball and tarot cards smarting and throbbing inside locked-up collections. Puppets and toys created far, far realer than they should be. Trees twisted with the force of something alien inside them. We are all over the world, we half-human sad, impregnated, lonely things, sung into life by magicians and pallid Hasids and evil PhDs who wanted to try and see— just try and see! they had wild hopes—if they could reproduce themselves without a partner.

The alchemists made their own little people out of chicken eggs mixed with human blood or sperm, bits of skin, occasionally animal hair or feathers. Sometimes dung (for who has not wished, at least once in their lives, to create a world out of their dung?) Other makers formed their creatures out of wood, or straw, or plastic that was enchanted so that it could think on its own, walk about, and have wishes.

I was one of these subtly manufactured little persons, one that canny old artist my mother had made, and I found her work in the stool-like shaping of myself—oh mother, forgive me!—disgusting.

When I was a child, she put her own art up in the kitchen, but never mine or my sisters'. She made male, earth-red masks from papier-mâché, fierce and staring, extraordinary. A painting that scared me (and I loved) of a tree with branches like claws, surrounded by a crying storm ("Mommy was having a very bad day when she made that."). A weird clown that looked like my father, sad and falsely smiling ("It's Daddy!" we cried happily). A still life of sensual apple, grapes, and pear that I thought was the most beautiful thing I

7

would ever see, and how amazing that I could see it every day while eating my peanut butter and jelly. A bad primitive watercolor of bleak houses and a tree by a lake. I thought all her art was genius then. Her output was prodigious. There was a needlepoint of her own face that depicted her as accurately as a photograph but also made her look exactly like the Virgin Mary.

Years later, there was a wild, abstract sculpture of her lungs, constructed of clear plastic tubing, with Aeolus, the god of the winds—a clay figure—attempting to breathe into them. (She was dying of lung disease.) A sexy, disturbing, luscious, Chinese-looking painting of a red rooster menacing a hen.

Then there was her writing. A ferocious story narrated by an insane boy who saw light all around him in wave form—I was eight, and it remains my favorite work by her. Her master's thesis on Feuerbach and Hegel—I was nine and I loved it, although I didn't know what "hermeneutics" were. Her dissertation on whether a Marxist philosophical framework might possibly allow for religion—I loved that, too, at fourteen, and was crushed when, at sixteen, she decided that her dissertation committee was too politically conservative to ever allow her to actually get her PhD on that topic, and so she transferred to Teachers College to produce a much tamer and more boring dissertation about Marxist pedagogy. I read all the drafts of all versions of the thesis and dissertation, and proofread them all, plus her translation from the Latin of Lucretius (my age: ten), and her undergrad Urban Planning paper (six) on the unique water supply of New York City. Don't even get me started on her poems.

I admired all of her art but I hated admiring it because it was always there, and it took up all our space. I also hated admiring it because my mother made me admire it, telling me her work was wonderful until it was the beginning and end of what I thought wonderful was.

When I was six, my mother asked if I wanted to be Haman for Purim and I thought that was a fantastically wonderful idea as well, because I had never been Haman and neither the girls nor boys had ever been him in my school; the girls were always Queen Esther in tinfoil crowns and kitchen-drapery ball gowns. I hated being Queen Esther, and I loved the idea of being someone evil.

Oh reader, assimilated or unknowing—no one dresses like Haman for Purim, for the simple reason that Haman is a genocidal murderer. Every Purim we celebrate that at the end of the Purim story, Haman's body has turned black and is hanging from the highest tree. We have put him there.

I certainly knew he was a genocidal monster when my mother dressed me up as him. My yeshiva was so Zionist that even the rabid Arab-hater Meir Kahane sent his daughter there, and my teachers were quite thorough on all points concerning violence against the Jews, even when addressing six year olds.

My mother worked so enthusiastically on my costume for Haman—sewing me a three-cornered (vinyl) dark purple hat, which functioned rather as Haman's SS helmet in the Purim story, putting one of her black wigs on my head to be Haman's hair, and another wig carefully cut to fit my face to be his beard. Outlining my brows and eyes in black pencil—that it was the best costume I have ever worn, and I hated every minute wearing it because it was all my mother's.

Nothing of the art of the Haman I was playing was me. Wearing the costume she had put together so artistically, I was simply being my mother's notion of Haman, my mother's transgression of gender and the niceties of Purim in my very conservative yeshiva, my mother's antic creature.

I have always hated being as porous as I am. Able to be filled with others' content. Mimsy—the portmanteau word Lewis Carroll coined for "flimsy" and "miserable" at once—unlocalizable, able to take any shape. Especially when directed by my mother ... Fey, impish, effeminate, will o' the wisp; mercurial, multifarious—counterfeit in my very being, like a photocopy of a human. Like those beautiful beings Puck and Ariel, who were really nothing more than great-looking, impressive slaves when you get right down to it. With them, as with me, there is no there there. All the creatures of Faerie are tricksy, thievish, prestidigitational performers. Fairies have the duplicity of all subject peoples.

I have always felt my own two-ness, always known that I was only half a person—if indeed that much. I realized very young that I was the true referent all those men unthinkingly have in mind when they refer to some gay man as a "lightweight" or a "Twinkletoes," someone who cannot fill his own, deep human shoes. I am the one they really meant. I have never been a real person; and I have always dissembled, or as my fairy kin like to say, beguiled. And I cannot help it, reader. Camus may have said "liberty is the right not to lie," but as for me, I have never been free.

And I hate it. I hate lying, which is the same as having no history, no will, and no capacity for connection with anyone. Liars do not speak the same language as friends, and therefore they cannot be friends.

Oh reader, hate me, put this down, throw me away, recycle me or even do it the old-fashioned way—burn me up in fire—but of course I love lying, too.

All my life I've been able to vanish quickly as a mouse, to borrow and not repay, to lie as lightly as a leprechaun. My mother taught me how to do all three. They form, in fact, almost the sum of the moral philosophy that she taught me. My progenitor was, not to put too fine a point on it, a professor of philosophy, and one of her most influential papers was a lesson plan for children about the goodness of lying, and the utter foolishness of every moral system that condemned it out of hand. For years, this curriculum was actually taught to public school children in New Jersey as a result of my mother's efforts. The proof of the lying lesson went like this. "You see your friend Stacey running away fast in one direction. When she is out of sight, a group of tough guys runs up to you, looking angry. Some of them are holding sticks and pipes. Their leader says, 'Where's that Stacey? We're so mad at her! We're gonna get her!' You point in the opposite direction from the way she ran. Did you do the right thing?"

My mother extended this to all other possible cases of lying. I had to lie to my aunt, to my grandparents—about things we had spent too much money on, or too little; where we had gone on vacation; the fact that I ate the free lunches offered by the city in my public school; the fact that my mother had told me, at age nine, what my aunt's first ten experiences of intercourse with her husband had been like (excruciatingly painful, but she persevered, and the eleventh was pleasurable). I had been at the wedding of Aunt Natalie and her husband Bernie, and it was both fun and discomfiting to know what their first intercourse experiences had been like.

And I had to lie to my sisters: "Don't tell Josie I said this," Mommy said, "but I happen to know that she is very, very jealous of you." I never told Josie my mother had warned me about this, but it influenced how I acted with Josie to the end of my days. To my other sister, Aphra, I could not reveal that my mother had said Aphra was a schizophrenic and "pathologically unable to separate from her."

My mother brought me with her to the New York Human Resources Administration (the city's welfare office), so that she would erroneously seem to be a poor single mother ("You always get more sympathy when you have a child with you," Mommy giggled). I was eight. We were lying and saying that Daddy didn't live with us and didn't share his income as a salesman or deliveryman with us. "No one can live on welfare and no other income," she told me, "it's too low. You have to lie."

In a sense she was certainly right. It is true that you couldn't live even the slightest bit well on welfare, including every family member buying books if they desired them, having the children go to camp—even at scholarship rates—in the summers, having meat—considered an important food for

11

children in the '60s and '70s—available several times a week.

(After a certain point in grad school my mother stopped cooking, but for years we ate costly TV dinners every night, with the so-called Hungry Man Dinner giving me a quivering butchy thrill as I ate the enormous roast-beef entree with its man-friendly apple cobbler, as often as I could get it.)

We shopped only at the really cheap clothing stores— Alexander's, Klein's, that pennyworth-apparel wonderland May's. But strangely, we sometimes went to Cape Cod for a two-week vacation. My mom said we were poor. (She made sure we had piano, singing, ballet and art lessons, either according to age—all six-year-olds in the family had to begin studying piano, for example—talent or inclination.)

My father worked alternately some lower-middle-class, working-class, and a few lumpen jobs (salesman for gates on stores, and by phone, for cemetery plots; deliveryman for Wise potato chips and later, crullers at 5:00 a.m. to greasy spoons; once, hander-out of fliers for a midtown sex parlor— "beautiful Asian masseuses" they said. My father, a silent man, didn't tell about the fliers; it was my mother who blabbed about them, gleefully).

The difference between her job as a philosophy-professor and his as a donut-deliverer (and pimp's helper) was the essence of my mother's mercurialness, her extreme mobility, and, she thought, her brilliance, her ability to turn dross into something shiny. She told my sisters and me that we were brilliant, too—everyone but my father, who she said was stupid and ugly and smelly—so that our splendid educations, including my mother's, came to seem the gold she had produced from the lead and dirty coal of my father's work by means of her own personal and unprecedented powers of alchemy.

My mother's work didn't produce very much income (as a professor, like many in our big-name city where instructors were supposed to live on prestige alone, she never made it above the adjunct stage), but it produced so much glory that, for my sisters and me, it was like looking at the Sun. The problem for us was that my father really *did* smell bad, not like a man who has gone to work and not yet showered but like a homeless person or a half-breed monster created by an evil magician and kept locked in the basement, its smell of rotting garbage occasionally rising above the extraordinary, magic sprays of air freshener and drowning them out.

I felt sorry for my little father-monster. I still do, for that smell he bore for his and my mother's experiments (was he her familiar? her assistant? her subject?) and that he still exudes from his plot in New Jersey, thirty years in the ground.

We had to put special chemicals in. My father had needed potentially toxic doses of preservatives and industrial wastes to keep him from simply decaying even in life, after the worst experiment had ended, the one where his tissues were interchanged with those of a female bear and he was baited for four years in a time-travel medieval English zoo, so that the already poisoned soil of New Jersey was deemed to be the only sustainable site for him when his time came.

My mother said none of me came from him, but I wonder.

Certainly I was more plastic than him. But did that make me more or less free? How can we say? I believe I had to lie more. My mother made me lie to my teacher—which hurt my positronic brain, or felt like it did, with the unbearable contradiction of Teachers as Not to Be Lied to and Teachers as Another Category to Be Bamboozled.

I was more nervous and ashamed of lying to my fifth grade teacher—about our address, as my mom demanded of me—than I have been nervous and ashamed about much else in my life. It felt like my body was burning on the inside and the outside to call out my fake address to my teacher, Mrs. Kay, when she was asking everybody's address for her file. I felt much worse on another day when she asked who needed a bus pass and I eagerly shot my hand up and Mrs. Kay asked for my address again and I had to give the fake one, only to have her chuckle sweetly and say, "Oh, that's only three blocks from school, you don't need to ride the bus, honey, do you?"

I had to smile painfully at her and affirm the lie.

But even more painful—surprisingly so—was the way my mother made me lie to Her Herself. My brain circuits bit into each other when I did that, and I would imagine the sharp edges of my internal motherboard rasping together. I was more intimate with my mother than I was with anybody else and, I thought, more intimate than I could be with anybody else. My mother made me, and she was my gazelle, my dove, my breathing supply, my Source. Reader, she was my only source of anything good—I had no other. I have perhaps neglected to say that she was beautiful. I have perhaps forgotten to tell you how she would kiss my face and say "You are my baby, my own one, my own!" She loved telling me stories that reflected her brilliance and, we both thought, my own, like "Poseidon Is Mad at Odysseus," or "Theseus Finds a Way Out of the Labyrinth Even Though Nobody Else Can!" She loved reading to me. She was my Sun, and yet I was supposed to lie to her.

This made me feel, at times, like I did not exist. This was a contradiction because she also told me that I did exist, through her—as her "brilliant baby." But mostly, what existed was the Sun, and everything else was a figment, like the shadows on Plato's (for of course we talked about Plato) cave wall.

She needed to think that I was constantly in a state of joy, perhaps because she was not. My mother worried about growing old, and she also worried about being ugly and disgusting with that pink and yellow and red and brown hole in her neck. It was odd and fragile, like a bit of cell wall that, under a microscope, resembles a little trove of flowers. But she kept it covered except at home, and no one mentioned it except, two or three times that I remember, my mother calling it "hideous" and "grisly."

But she would ask, "Is my nose bigger than that other witch's over there? And whose wrinkles are bigger, mine or hers?" And, as I said, my mother was convinced she was dying ever since the 1971 operation, and would call Doctors on Call—doctors you had never met before that you could pay to come to the house on an hour's notice. The clean-scrubbed young doctors would arrive with beefy bodyguards with guns (this was the '70s), and the doctors brought immense black doctors' bags of Valium and Demerol with them, which they would give my mother. She called them every month or so.

When she had her original surgery, I dreamed that my mother was a car, and my father, sisters and I were all driving in her. I was afraid that my father was driving her too fast, and then he *was* driving her too fast—and she needed an operation. And so my father performed a tracheotomy with his pocketknife, through the roof of the car. In real life, this is what my mother had—a permanent tracheotomy, which was now the only organ through which my mother was able to breathe. In my dream she had a permanent slit through her own roof.

She was afraid, as I have said, of dying. But she was even more scared of being beaten in some even more dreadful and systematic way, being taken advantage of, being humiliated like someone who had never even been a philosopher. Of being smashed up like someone who was not even the weakest wizard. Being made mock of and *kicked*, like someone who didn't even have a brain.

Many years later, when I had begun to study karate at twenty-one and was showing my moves around the house, she kicked me in the shins because she assumed (incorrectly) that I was going to hit her.

As a child, of course, I did not take karate, because ecstatic pointy-headed goblin-toys do not require it. Though she did partly want me to be happy for my own sake, my mother mainly believed that toys are here to sing and entertain, to throw themselves in the air and then catch themselves, in ridiculous clothes like jesters. Sad jesters are hardly effective, and no one wants sad or angry toys, either. I have quite a lot of toys here on my desk as I write this, and not a one of them has ever told me that we need to talk, or that they had an accident and wet their pants, or that they sometimes got scared at night.

I loved my Sun-like mother, but I hated showing her only this half of myself. It often made me feel like I didn't possess even the barest strip of reality that I thought I did, that I was the most basic schematic drawing of myself and not even the actual fully-produced android.

And whenever my sister Josie was unhappy, my mother would prepare a little suitcase. She would pack it and bring it downstairs to our dimly-lit apartment house lobby, and Josie would have to wait with it, crying, for a car my mother had presumably called that would take her away.

In the end my mother would always forgive her and allow her to stay. But I didn't know she would, and Josie didn't, either. I never had my suitcase packed; I was too good a schematic drawing for that. I have always been good at what I do; I would never let my mother see me as unhappy as Josie let herself be seen. I was very proud of this. For years my mom and I played a game called "Smart Baby" where, in the game, I began life as smart as an adult, already knowing how to read and write and do sums and every other task that grown-up people did. I knew history, and geography, and science. As my mother put it, I already knew everything and could do everything. I needed nothing.

A few times, when my sisters and I had let down our guard and actually allowed *my mother* to become unhappy, she packed a big suitcase—her own—and said she was going to leave. She did in fact leave two or three times during our childhood for a night or two (because "I just have to get away"), although more often my sisters and I won her over when we begged her to stay.

She liked me to amuse her with word games and displays

of my many mental talents. For her friends, at dinner parties, she would have me read my poems and book reports and personal declarations (like "This Is Why I Am Now Sure That God Cannot Be Both Omnipotent and Good").

She had me declaim aloud to her friends the poems of other people that I liked, like Edna St. Vincent Millay telling a bird who represented Thought to "Depart, be lost. /But climb."

You might have anticipated, reader, that so big a ham as I would have loved this exhibition, but I feared and hated it. It made me sad because it wasn't me; even though it entailed reciting things I had written or poems that I liked, it wasn't me back then to show off and entertain with them. None of it was my desire, not even the desire to entertain, at the beginning. Reader, if you can imagine a Puck who is secretly depressed, who worries in the bathroom and sneaks off to smoke and smash his toes into the hard, white tile wall, that Puck was me.

Reader, I had difficulties from my mother creating me out of whole cloth, but I had even more from my father's surreal sports, employing me as the birdie in his games of badminton.

Using me as the pins and ball (and sometimes the alley and the next lane) in his games of bowling.

Using me as the puck (yes, my reader, the Puck, the two have always been connected) in his games of field hockey.

Using me as the ball and clubs and beret in his games of golf.

Using me as the ball in his games of jai alai.

How his perceptions could become so altered that he could think I was a piece of state-of-the-art athletic equipment, bought at a nearby mall, I do not know. I do know his perceptions were very altered. (Mine would be, if I'd been bear-baited, for sure.)

Reader, my father hit me, and the rhyme or reason to it was as frankly odd as if he had instead played Ultimate Frisbee with my cheeks, or used my gallbladder as a mallet in a gentlemen's game of croquet. He was not—as I hope I have made crystal clear—a dominant force in my family, and yet he was allowed a certain liberty to use my brows as bocce-balls and my temples as a wiffle ball, however many times he wanted.

My mother didn't mind. Sometimes he hit me when she wasn't there, sometimes when she was, but it did not matter as long as he did not strike me many blows at a time, in which case she would tell him huffily, "That's enough." But, reader, even his single blows were enormous, like a giant's, and his short recreations hurt me.

Perhaps I've lied. It wasn't only recreational for him to strike me—I clearly made him angry, although it was often surprising what made him angry at me on any particular occasion.

He was sensitive. And my mother added to his pool of sensitivity daily, by saying things like, "You're just too stupid to understand!" in everybody's earshot. He never talked back to her when she said things like that. She also told jokes to which my father was the punch line—"What's immovable and fat and hairy and idiotic?" and encouraged my sisters and me to make fun of him. I only once saw him reading a book—*My Name Is Asher Lev* by Chaim Potok—and clearly the only possible thing for me to do was to say, "Holy Christ, Daddy's reading a book! What if his brain pushes out of his head?"

But he did not strike me when I said that. I don't remember which words of mine made him do it. He smelled so unbearably bad that we made some playful jokes at his expense about emergency deliveries of Odor Eaters, but he did not hit me (or my sisters, who for some reason he never hit) in response to that, but to other things that I really, really can't remember, reader. Were they innocent things like "Would you mind leaving me some of the pickles?" Or mean things like "I'd never be as stupid as you!"

Whatever I said to inspire him is lost in the fog that always overcame me at such moments, which has made me remember them utterly differently from all other events in my long life. Not as discrete happenings, but as one long, never-fading, continually present moment of getting hit (like a robot programmed to see a giant fist coming down on its head every nanosecond, so it must scurry to come up with a million strategies of avoidance, as long as its power is on).

I did frequently call him stupid. But so did he call me. He never acted like my father, not remotely. We were always equals in the Minkowitz Family Consortium, except that he was four times my size and had a vastly stronger arm. My mother treated him like just another child in the family, albeit the one who was supposed to be hated.

I was seven when he started, and he always hit my head.

It hurt. And reader, it made me terrified in a peculiar way, of everything under the sun, and all creatures that flew in the air, and ones that crept on the earth, of all people and, of course, games engaged in by the arms.

For years, the sound of keys disturbed me, I had no idea why. I think now that it was the sound of his keys in the door. I do know I was frightened whenever he was home, and felt safe when he was not.

My plasticity came in handy, I think, because it made it easier for me to assume the roles as the equipment in the ballgames than a non-goblin individual would have found it. I was made of Things, after all, reader, a variety of largely inorganic and inhuman Things, and being treated as a thing could not have made as big an impression on me as it would have on a biological girl. Soil and paper and nails do not feel as much as humans do, and have never done. Not even muffin batter, the nearest thing I have to human flesh, and which I have only in a very small amount, feels anything like what human beings feel. This is the reason Rabbi Judah Loew was allowed to make a golem in the first place, and the reason he was allowed to destroy it, as Abraham was not allowed to destroy his son

CHAPTER 2

The only problem was that I was ambitious.

Even golems have ambitions, little reader—perhaps you think we didn't? You probably think that slaves are happy, and dwarves don't mind being tossed, and beings named Jack are fond of popping out of their boxes when their little crank is cranked. But as far back as high school (for even androids go to high school, if they require educating, and if their mad scientist-inventors insist on it), I had read the *Village Voice*, and wistfully, oh, so utterly wistfully, dreamed that I might someday write for it.

Golems do not usually write for the *Village Voice*, reader. People assume we don't have the creativity or the independence. People think we lack the necessary confidence, that pure human *cojones*. Homo sapiens' sense of superiority gives even human women the balls and swagger necessary to tell other people what they think all the time in print. I had no *cojones* at all, nor even any human genes (unless my mother did cut her fingernails for me) to contravene my android weakness, my basic pallidness. My lack of a spirit blown into me by God.

But the *Village Voice* itself was not a pure or normal institution in those days, and did not care a fig for God, or human beings' sense of superiority. It didn't even really care a jot about testicles. This was 1979—the peak of my high school days, reader. It was not a law-abiding time on any of the populated planets. The Shah of Iran was overthrown in 1979. The Nicaraguans reamed General Anastasio Somoza a new one in 1979. In 1979, the filming of the movie *Cruising* was disrupted by angry, screaming gay men and lesbians (very few people had even knowingly seen angry, screaming gay men and lesbians before). The Venusians stopped mining their own sex-crystals for their overlords, and the Alpha Centaurians rioted over the suppression of irrational numbers. Other newspapers did not reflect the burningness and liberation of those times, but the *Voice* did. I had begun to get interested in the paper even as far back as 1977, 1976, for the *Village Voice* was funky, a cauldron, a kettle of truly rich, weird soup, and concerned with the most unusual bodies and minds in the universe.

A strange lesbian named Jill Johnston wrote articles that I could not read because they had no punctuation or even paragraph divisions, but that I admired anyhow because she got away with writing that weird way, and with saying that she loved having sex with women and not men. A man named Arthur Bell, the *Voice's* first gay-rights reporter, wrote columns that were far more conventional in form, but that I read eagerly anyhow because they were pumped full of an anger toward straight people that was similar to the stark anger I had often felt towards the human-born.

I didn't know before then that anyone was actually allowed to express anger toward the normal folks. Back then, I wasn't even homo myself. (It's doubtful, in any case, whether you could even say I had the "same" sex as the non-clay, biological humans to whom I was eventually attracted. Human vulvas are not the same as dust-and-magic vulvas.) But I flipped first to the *Voice's* homo pages anyhow because they were so courageously perverse. Then I flipped second to the personal ads, where people wrote oddly and beautifully about their own unusual and beautiful, sexual and emotional needs. (This was a far cry from today's cookie-cutter personal ads, reader, which have no literary value and no soul. Personal ads were glorious then, even radical, and the *Voice* was their hot, true home!)

The hetero and homo ads were both radical in those years. It was new for people to say what they wanted, and—therefore!?—they allowed what they wanted to be truly new, surprising to themselves and others. "Cock and ball torture now!... Invent new rituals with me. Be my six-foot-tall bunny-monster, and I'll be your beautiful forest.... Brainy, quiet but restless bi male seeks F or M for walking, conversation only... So, here's the deal: I'll push you away, and then you'll get cold and distant. You know you want to! Let's do it! Box 2154... I deeply value love, pussy, and music... Write a sestina for me and I'll get you so high you can't see straight."

I read these all, every week. I was eleven years old. We lived in Coney Island, across the street from the ocean, our eighth apartment in eleven years. It was a poor and dangerous neighborhood, the poorest and most dangerous that I ever lived in, to which my mother had apparently moved us because she thought the apartments in a new affordable-housing project there were spacious and pretty. Packs of emaciated and scarred stray dogs moved through the streets together, biting each other or sometimes, it seemed, fucking. ("Fucking" was the word used most often in my family, because my mother, as a magician, believed in using the most potent words always.) I had to do the grocery shopping every day, but I was scared of the packs of dogs and of the winos who made noises at me through the sides of their mouths, from the alleyways. The newspaper said that girls had been raped under the boardwalk, two blocks from our house. The day we moved in, boys from our project threw rocks at us, smashing my bedroom mirror.

One night, I was lying in bed trying to sleep, with my door open in the summer heat. I heard my parents whisper low, and then my father yell suddenly loudly and with hate, "SHE'S LISTENING!! SHE'S LYING THERE LISTENING TO US! SHE'S LISTENING!" He was murderously angry at me, I was startled to realize, because he thought I was somehow trying to listen to my parents having sex. I didn't understand what they were talking about until my father yelled his fury at me. I closed my door, furiously embarrassed and frightened.

That year I also remember feeling sorry for my father for the first time, because I had begun to do the family laundry sometimes and I was able to see his socks and underwear.

The rest of our family's socks were fine, but my father's socks made me terribly sad. They were shrunken things, far too small for him, with sticky stains in the toes. Little crumpled jots of polyester, and full of holes. As for his underwear, they were holey, too, but the main thing that made me sad was they were streaked with yellow lines and perhaps a few brown ones.

Why did he take care of himself so badly?

I decided to try to investigate my father, figure out why he was the way he was. People often kept secret things in their underwear drawers. So one day when no one else was home, I went into their fancy master bedroom and invaded his. Under the briefs, among the grieving socks, I pulled out two paperbacks:

(I'd never seen him read, except *Asher Lev* that one time.) One was called *Hot for Pain*. The other little paperback was *Miss Kitty's Disciplining School*. I read them, sitting on my parents' bed. I'd hardly ever been in my parents' bedroom before, in our eight apartments. I still remember how fancy it was, with a modern, brown-wood bedroom set and a trio of pointy mirrors over the dresser. My parents had the fanciest furniture in the house.

I sat on the bed, which smelled of Lemon Pledge, and read my father's books.

Hot for Pain was about a man who disciplined a set of women by whipping them and sticking his penis in them. *Miss Kitty's Disciplining School* was about a woman, Miss Kitty, who kept calling a man named slave a "worm" and hitting him

23

across the ass with a riding crop.

The books turned me on, especially one of them, far more than the other. It is a point of great perplexity for me that I can no longer remember which of them turned me on more. I do remember I could not find it sexy to be called a "worm." I had never, ever been turned on by reading before and it was upsetting to be excited by scenes of men and women getting hit. (I was only eleven and could count on three fingers the number of times I had been turned on before.) It was even more upsetting that my father presumably was excited, too.

Was he excited when he hit me? The possibility terrified me. Was he more excited when he was hitting or being hit? Who was my father, exactly, and why did he never talk to me?

Although people wrote personal ads seeking that kind of sex in the *Voice*, it was my mother, not my father, who brought home the *Voice* for us. The *Voice* actually cost money in those days, but we willingly paid for it—it was the best periodical around, except for maybe the *New Yorker*, which was outside our acquaintance, probably because of class. I started out reading mostly the personal ads—sometimes my sisters and my mom and I would read them aloud together, laughing. Aphra, seventeen, liked reading Jill Johnston, and would keep Jill's lesbo treatises on the kitchen table and say how much she loved them.

By fourteen, I myself was more in love with Jeff Weinstein and Ellen Willis. Ellen Willis wrote about her desires, even if they were ugly or unfeminine or antisocial or disturbingly self-undermining. She was fearless in a way that neither male writers nor feminists had been to that point; she ruthlessly exposed her own contradictions. Willis wrote that she could not simply dismiss the Sex Pistols' sexist and nasty anti-abortion song, "Bodies," although it was, she said, "an outburst of loathing for human physicality, a loathing projected onto women because they have babies and abortions

24

and are 'a fucking bloody mess' [as the Sex Pistols put it]."
She could not just dismiss the song, she wrote, because "the
extremity of its disgust forced me to admit that I was no
stranger to such feelings."

I couldn't believe anyone would admit they had
disturbing and terrifying feelings that undermined their own
deepest strength.

I *only* had feelings of that kind, and I did not plan on
broadcasting it. None of my feelings were connected to my
source of strength, because golems are bred for self-disgust
and a permanent discipline.

Still, the *Voice's* restaurant reviewer, Jeff Weinstein, did
not seem to be disgusted by anyone or anything. He could
even love food products that had actually been manufactured
in factories. On one occasion, Jeff wrote a sensual and moving
review of a canned spray that smelled exactly like the scent of
a warm, buttery apple pie.

He quoted Keats in order to praise that apple pie spray.

That review spoke to me. Did not sprays have their
poetry, too, and the tormented aluminum beings their own
beating hearts?

I lived in the world of poetry, despite having some
industrial garbage in me and even some chemical food
preservatives that, drying, had helped to form my faux-
skeleton. Why couldn't a spray can hang out at Max's Kansas
City and drink beers, and write its own occasional poetry, too?

Some people had mind-blowing sex with their TVs, so
why should it be inconceivable that a being like me, a sort of
extra-thoughtful, extra-passionate toaster, was capable of
love?

Fuck.

There is—oh reader—inevitably—something more that
I'm not saying. A thing I have to mention before I tell you
what happened to my arms, and with the married woman, and
the rest of this terrible story. It sticks in my throat.

Or it inheres in the skin under my skin—I have always

25

been quite confused about what kind of things are my body, and what kind of things *aren't it*—what my mother attached to me with the extra glue left over at the end—how far my body extends into the world, and which objects are actually embedded in it and which are other than me.

So: in the organs beneath my first layer of cleverly shaped imitation-human organs, in the old sheep-caul membrane she stitched inside as an extra structure on which to hang all that painted work (the taxidermy and papier-mâché that form my base), with nickels and Lifesavers and Christmas ornaments embedded here and there to spark the magic, there is an activity that does not like to describe itself.

But I will tell you what it is.

My mother put locks on her speech, on my speech, even the speech of some little gnomes and watchful ghosts we had around the house, but I have found a way to pick them all. I already told you I'm a good liar. I'm pretty swell at cheating at cards, lock-picking, and escaping, too.

I am covered with oil; you cannot keep me tied. I am Houdini. I am Proteus.

My mother—I feel stupid now for all the suspense, you probably won't even find this a big deal—why am I breaking out the good olive oil for this? You'll probably just think that I'm a huge baby—well, she used to do things that turned me on sexually.

It confused me. And ignited me. Both those things happened when my mother danced out in front of me with no clothes on, or in her most ecstatic panties, silk nothings tied with bows, or else exquisitely see-through red or black—filmy and beautiful—asking, "Don't I look sexy?"

She would model nightly for me and my sisters. There was a bra of fire-colored lace through which the cleavage was a heaven that I tried not to look at. There was a gorgeous blouse-and-pants set with an Edenic apple tree stretching wide across her breasts, a set my mother was wearing when, she told us delightedly, a man had mistaken her for a prostitute and asked how much she cost. The prostitute-mistaking had happened that very afternoon.

The new clothes and the modeling began right after my mother's surgery, when the new hole had been carved into the bottom of her neck. Her nose and mouth had been disconnected from her breathing apparatus. Perhaps this was the reason why she seemed to have become an entirely different person. For a few months my mother was only able to eat disgusting-looking, foul-scented foods she prepared for herself in the blender—spinach or chicken or liver puree, along with actual jars of baby food. I was much younger then—only seven—and my mother had suddenly changed her wardrobe and all her customs around dressing and undressing. She showed herself naked to us kids for the first time, and her newly-seen body seemed white-hot. No one in my family had gone naked to the others before then, except (presumably) my mother and father. Now my mother showed off her nipples to me, smiling as I watched. They were large and brown, luscious and disturbing to me.

She wore a tiny yellow sundress that made her look exactly like the hillbilly dreamboat Daisy Mae in the Li'l Abner Sunday comic that I read each week with lust and confusion. Daisy Mae looked skanky but lovely, and her so-deep cleavage gave her a confusing, shameful power over all the men.

I began to have a new job, every afternoon: washing my mother's back in the bathtub. I never questioned why it was my job and not, say, my father's, but I came to sit on the tub whenever my mother summoned me, dreading it. I was supposed to wash her back to prevent her from drowning, my mother said. She was afraid of accidentally getting water into her new "hole" if she washed herself. (Why she thought a seven-year-old would be better at not getting water there, I do not know.)

My mother washed all of her other parts herself, including her lustrous long black hair. But her back—with creamy freckles all over it, a beautiful back, as my mother always told us, was for me to wash with a washcloth. I cannot remember any more paralyzing moment from my childhood than entering that bathroom and trying to avoid looking at my mother's breasts. Or her vagina from under the waters, its hair gone smooth and luxuriant. I would cross that enormous expanse—from the bathroom door through the entire front side of my mother—and finally get to the back, which was less frightening but still too creamy and beautiful. I tried not to look at any other part of my mother but her back. I told my mother I didn't like washing her back, but she said I had to or she would drown. I finally stopped doing it, perhaps by fourteen.

As a result, reader: I was not used to having what I wanted. I was used to longing for what I needed and never, ever getting it. To staring at what I needed shamefaced, from the other side of the bathroom, in fear and regret and love and pain.

All golems have faced immediate death at every moment, because their makers could kill them by writing just one letter of the alphabet on their bodies, or erasing one. By telling them to die, a command that every golem must obey; by pulling a holy scrap of paper out of their mouths, on which a secret name of God had been written; or by walking around the golem three times and saying God's names backwards.

So I was terrified, each time I came close to anything I needed, that it was going to be snatched from me like my mother snatching the life-conferring paper out of my mouth. My ticket being snatched. Dying again, the way I did every afternoon washing my mother's back.

Given a hope of living, and then frustrated.

CHAPTER 3

I have always understood that I had to use special means to get ahead, as a non-human with a divided self. (Half of myself was Mom's, and half my own.) I had special deficits, I knew—the very opposite of superpowers. Don't ever put me near a flame, because I'd go up like a straw doll soaked in kerosene; don't tap me even lightly on a special panel in the middle of my back, because that would turn me off until you chose to turn me on again. I had to lie as hard as I could so that no one ever found out.

So when I first came down to the *Village Voice* at twenty-two, I took over one of the two "free" computers intended for all freelancers, seized it as my own. I'd put my files and my coffee cup there, my own guerrilla seizure just like Fidel or Che. Everything I did felt like a revolutionary appropriation to me then, or some sort of theft. I was the best freeloader in Brooklyn. I would sponge $20 from a friend with no intention of paying it back ($20 in '80s dollars, that is), or bagels and hummus and salad from the buffet of a conference I was not attending. I used my sister Josie's credit card, with her permission but no intention of paying her back on time. Since she made more money than me, I thought it was fine to make her lay it out until I paid her. If you want to know my mindset, think of my kinsman the Gingerbread Man, running and successfully getting away from all those sets of lips and teeth.

When another freelancer objected to my taking over the computer—only one ever did, though sad to say it was the one who later won the Pulitzer—I played dumb. "Yeah, that's my stuff," I said politely, smiling. "Oh, is it not supposed to be there? I'm sorry." But I'd kept it there.

I needed my own recognized place at the *Voice*, and I also needed what that place would signify: that I was a "real" and legitimate writer for the paper, one who was entitled to a private desk and phone line. I pretended that I had these already; I expropriated them, or, to use my favorite phrase, I "liberated" them. There was a phone line at the "free" computer; I told the *Voice* phone operator to put my calls through to me at that extension, and it became "my" phone line.

Folks like me have always had to be good at acting. All the golems in Jewish history had been ordered to dress up as *goyim* in order to investigate who was behind the blood libels. (Of course, the golems had had to pretend to be human beings in the first place, even before they put on their special *goyim* suits.) Previously I had pretended things because my mother forced me to, but now I was acting for my own purposes. I knew nothing about reporting, not even that one ought to tell the truth.

My mother had taught me that truth is a matter of fighting for one's interests, not revealing secrets for nothing. The Gingerbread Man became my model: he looked like a person and so effectively *became* a person, until someone finally caught and ate him.

My plan was to write for the *Voice* as much as I could until that happened.

Soon—as they say in bountiful 12-step—I "acted as if" I should be given a column. The *Voice*, ridiculously, obliged! The column was called "Body Politics." Oh, if you insist on holding me to petty accuracies I must reveal that I shared the column, alternate weeks, with a cantankerous and talented sea-monster named Richard Goldstein. Richard, seventy-three feet long and colored orange with big, unpleasant, gray constricting coils down the length of his body, was my editor. Everyone else was afraid to work with him. Everything gay in content had to get past Richard before it could be allowed into the paper, and he was a terrifying guardian. He was also a brilliant writer in his own right, but he didn't start writing about Gay Love till I was in college, when I read him for the first time and wanted to lick his throat and hands for hours. I didn't know he was a sea-monster and didn't have a throat or hands! His writing was so good that I would have sucked his monstrous coils.

Richard was rather like my mother but with a penis, and with less narcissism about his personal appearance. He was the most dominant person I have ever met, but then, at 22 I was most accustomed to interacting with dominant and terrifying persons, and it was probably more comfortable for me to go into Richard's office and have him wrap his tentacles around me and squeeze, than it would have been to have a gentle, kindly editor.

I wooed him—this was the word I always used for what I did with Richard—I was a persistent suitor, once I'd found out he was the Cerberus of Gaydom, and I wooed him with the fierce young demonstrators in my articles, hot boys and girls from the Free Queer States, radical commentary and doggie treats until he sighed, contented, like a mesmerized hogfish, and rolled over.

My power to sing Richard to sleep was only partial, of course. Sometimes he would lick story ideas from my hands slowly and rhythmically for hours only to stir suddenly and leap ferociously for my throat. The copy editors and fact-checkers hated him because they were the least powerful people at the paper and he was rude to them, kept them waiting for hours, and often prevented them from doing their jobs on pieces he had written or edited, overruling them in the exercise of the only authority they had. The copy editors and fact-checkers were mostly my age (I had been a freelance copy editor in their ranks during the whole time I'd wooed Richard) and they were all also writers, but unlike me had won over no monster-editor to their side. I would smile inside whenever Richard was rude to them, feeling the cosmic joy of being preferred by a parental sea-monster who was nasty and hurtful to all the other children.

I flattered myself that he was never nasty and hurtful to me. In fact, he was—many times—but I trained myself assiduously not to notice. I told myself that I knew how to talk to Richard, knew how to endure him and how to deal with him, because we had both had particularly unpleasant spells put on us by our parents. Richard had told me about his own underwater childhood less than a year into our writer-editor relationship. First, my mentor had told me a piece of news about myself that shocked me.

"You're obsessed with violence in your writing," Richard told me, after I had turned in a piece about a lesbian who had taken her lover, who'd just been raped, to the emergency room, only to be set on by hospital security guards who dyke-baited the couple and beat the crap out of both of them. It wasn't just the subject of the piece, which was my first large article for the *Voice*. It was the graphic—almost pornographic—quality of the writing, where I mentioned every bruise on the rape victim's lover, how many inches each had measured, according to her doctor, how her lover, who'd been anally raped, had been sitting in the emergency room covered with shit.

Reader, I took it as my duty to report on the size and location of the bruises and how many times they hit her because I was afraid no one would react with enough outrage. I was afraid people wouldn't think what had happened was as bad as all that. You could say I was responding like a golem, protecting my community from the pogrom that encircled it.

In fact, after the *Voice* published the article, ACT UP demonstrated inside the entrance to the emergency room where the employees had beaten up the women. Four hundred people chanted at the top of their lungs inside that entrance, and left the wooden statue of Jesus on the wall covered in Silence = Death stickers. It was as though I myself had summoned a golem, a golem named ACT UP, that had toddled into the hospital and, with the weight of its enormous body on the floors, made St. Vincent's quake.

The hospital initiated reforms after that.

St. Vincent's was the main medical facility in the Village, and the place where most people with AIDS went then when they were ill.

It was only after the article had been published that I considered the fact that the rape victim's lover was an extremely belligerent, indeed a violent person who just may have started the fight. It didn't make the guards' assault on the couple less outrageous and unjust, just less telling about the utter egregiousness of homophobia at the hospital.

(Actually, a few years later, the lover, who'd been so impressed by how powerful a golem ACT UP was that she joined the group, threatened me at the crowded ACT UP meeting. I'd said "Shh!" to her when she was talking loudly and I could not hear the speaker. "Don't ssh me!" she yelped. "If you know what's good for you.")

When Richard informed me back in 1988 that I was obsessed with violence, I took a deep breath.

"You're right," I said, and began to think about all of the other reported pieces, essays and poems I had written about violence. There were at least 380 of them in the years since I had first started writing in sixth grade. I wrote a column called "Body Politics," after all, because I knew what it was like to have a body that had been shaped to serve. My different, actionable, pressable, queer body had been, I believe, badly battered by the very process that created it—not by being made gay, Lord knows! but by being made with a body that my owner intended to control. It is nauseating just to inhabit a body designed to do the will of another, and the vertigo I experienced whenever my mother moved my parts for me made it hard to touch the soul that was inside me.

33

My joints were weird, scalloped, and vulnerable, like the ones on the G.I. Joe I had gotten as a hand-me-down from my mother's little brother Henry. The G.I. Joe had long joint-holes in his wrists, neck, ankles, knees, and elbows, which, at nine, I could think of only one thing to do with—torture him. I put knives and pen points in his joint-holes, one by one, lovingly, relishing what I imagined it was doing to him.

As an action figure myself, I had felt the same. In point of fact, all action figures feel vertigo when people move their parts around, playing with them.

My father had moved my parts for me, too, when he hit them, rather like the New York State prison guards I'd also written about who had manipulated the parts of a man imprisoned on the Special Inmates Block until he died. (Those who play with marionettes have to be fanatically careful, or they just fall apart.)

The Special Inmates Block at the upstate prison in Clinton, New York was for mad, developmentally disabled, or simply distraught inmates. The guards would amuse themselves by smacking the prisoners all day, and posting jokes and cartoons about hitting people on their bulletin board. ("Beetle Bailey" has an awful lot of jokes about Sarge beating the shit out of Beetle, so it was the guards' favorite.)

My poor father had in fact been imprisoned in a kind of Special Inmates Block at a U.S. military stockade in Hamburg, Germany. I didn't know very much about it, but according to my mother he'd been put there because he had "gone crazy" and beat up his own sergeant, after the sergeant had kept calling him a dirty Jew.

I was eight when my mother told me. By happenstance, there was a book in our living room at the time called *Military Justice Is to Justice As Military Music Is to Music* and I read it cover to cover in the bathroom, passionate to know about him. The book said that for decades, U.S. soldiers in U.S. military prisons had been brutally beaten daily, as a matter of policy.

My father never spoke of any of it.

At the *Voice* I lived to punish police and prison guards, and anyone anywhere who fractured people's bodies. I wrote about sexual abuse, rape, baby- and wife-beating. I created article after article out of what Lenin—a journalist originally!—called "exposures," revelations of horrible things that were being done to human beings, and must stop (as he put it so eloquently in his essay "Can a Newspaper Be a Collective Organizer?" 1902.)

But mostly I wrote about being queer, because that was a good metaphor for my own extreme physical disenfranchisement. My body was supposed to do the will of others, not its own. Like Pinocchio's body, made of trees, it was supposed to obey, and never play. Pinocchio was told that if he obeyed completely he would finally be allowed to be a real boy, but as for me, I doubted (despite Lenin, despite what I was able to accomplish with St. Vincent's) that I could ever be real.

CHAPTER 4

Hamlet was very likely also a magic action figure that someone had enchanted. Why else would he say, "Oh that this too, too solid flesh would melt"? The bespelled flesh was too disgustingly solid to let him float away into the world of Play, where he should have been allowed to stay in the first place. It is very magic-action-figure, in any case, to think of life as a "coil" that one itches to take off.

My own body was also stuck between the worlds. It was neither fish nor fowl; it belonged neither to me nor, anymore, to others.

My father had died in my freshman year of college, of a sudden cancer. He wasn't around to read all my exposures of the prison guards, no matter how many of them I made. And my dad, a concerned Jew underneath all his enchantments, wasn't around to rejoice in my beating back the pogroms. As for my mother, now that I lived on my own I wasn't sure whether she still owned my body, but she seemed to command it from afar by remote control. What was that line from Emily Dickinson? "The absence of the witch does not/Invalidate the spell." Anyhow, I still saw my mother all the time. I allowed my body to go inside her house, and allowed hers inside my own.

My own. *My* body: sometimes it seemed I could command it for five seconds—10—maybe 15 if I pushed it, but no longer than that. Nor did my father's sudden absence invalidate the spells he'd unknowingly cast on me himself, from the poor witless isolation of his foul juju'd monsterhood.

But his dying cut the legs out from under my family. When the fast, brutal lung cancer had eaten him through in about eight months, I was surprised to find I'd lost some kind of bulwark in him, my ogre. Somehow, he had been my mainstay against my mother. Because he was male, or because he wasn't her, or perhaps because he was the thing she hated, I felt almost as though I'd lost my dick.

I had found my father's cancer pretty pleasant at first because he had lost a lot of weight and had gotten much less frightening. He was now a pale, thin man like a piece of white asparagus from Europe, even his face no longer red like a meat slab with an anger problem. In the mild spring of my senior year of high school, I could come home from school and not be afraid if he was in the house.

When my father was closer to death it was a little different. Beyond losing the particular person he was (who was that?), whom I found it acutely painful suddenly not to have known, he'd been a wedge against falling into her completely.

Now, as I became the first golem in history to go to school at Yale, I was ashamed to discover that the loss of my father's Minkowitz role was almost as great a loss as that original loss of *him*. With him gone, my family members found that we had lost a placeholder, a hate object, someone to cushion us against the realities of our bizarre family situation.

Never mind that he was part of our bizarre family situation—he was, more saliently for the rest of us, a cushion, a bit of armchair stuffing, a shock absorber. Everything started to hurt more with him gone, as though he had been a nice pillow shoring up the space against the impact of my mother. Even my mother felt this stuffing gap, I believe. Our family life began to be unstable, with open fights breaking out suddenly between the members and naked statements of doubt, and rage.

Now, in our post-high school years, my mother began suddenly to give my sisters and me way too generous gifts, as if to win us by other means now that Daddy wasn't around to provide a comparison, a distraction. She had been so much better than my father that I'd *had* to love her.

Maybe my mother's new kind of gifts were to make up for the past. They were some sort of supplement, whether for my father's loss or for having to put up with him I wasn't sure.

I think my mother secured her future as best she could by adapting. Well, perhaps that is too cold an assessment of it. My mother changed. Maybe she felt guilty. In a way it was just an extension of her extravagant manner of our childhoods, when she'd overwhelmed us telling us the plots of porno movies she'd just been to see ("the semen on her face cured the girl's acne!"), and exuberant kisses that always left sexy lipstick imprints on me like the ones adult men are supposed to get on their collars.

Now she was pouring out humdrum objects to win us. My mother had never been humdrum before, but suddenly she was like the mother on a cake-mix box, flooding us with homely necessities like socks, comfy robes, Dr. Dentons (those old-fashioned girls' pajamas with the feet attached, given to us as adult women), chaste television cozies from L. L. Bean (a cross between a sweater and a blanket, for feeling safe while watching TV), warm flannel clothing for exercising or frolicking with squirrels, nothing remotely sexy, everything providing snugly comfort.

These motherly gifts were a shock of joy for me. The cotton softness of it all was ecstatic, like a wedding after a war, like finding yourself with a leg that had been missing from birth and jumping up and down on it to play with its impossible support. I felt five years old every Christmas now, opening presents and gazing back at my mother with a joy that felt nearly criminal. There were colorful but nicely butch women's nightshirts in bright red and blue, down booties, warm sleep caps in case I got cold. My gift pile was enormous and tied with beautiful bows, wrapped in paper with Santas or Disney characters, sometimes candy canes. The stack would feel like her mother love in wholesome, huge, emphatic form, a tad aggressive in its size and scale perhaps, but appropriate, I felt, given the insufficient and degraded versions of it I'd experienced before. She was now the source of all my sleep clothes, so she was there every night right next to my dreaming and to that quick moment of trust you have to have just before you plunge into unconsciousness.

My mother also gave me lots of little payments that I began to ask for in my 20s, starting from the time I began at the *Voice*. I thought of them, when I thought of them at all, as reparations, sometimes punitively but often in a friendly sense, as though they were a simple restoration, almost the repair of an oversight. When my bank account ran out, which happened frequently because I paid no attention to it, I would stop by.

I would usually ask for $100—in a check signed with my mother's sweet signature. I would always get it. It seemed like a small amount to me. Around 32 or so, I continued to ask for money, but I began to treat it as a loan and I'd repay it—with a little interest, even. Except, of course, just four years later, when my arms suddenly broke and I began to feel like a poor person again, the most golem like of golems and incapable of repaying anything.

Before that happened—my mother and I had fights, but I was so glad to get her new, big, hot love that I always came back. She clipped every single one of my articles from the *Voice* and any other venue I was published in, read it and saved it. She wrote an indignant letter to the *New York Times Book Review* when I was once criticized in its pages. I was pleased, but didn't let her mail it because in the letter she called my writing "penetratingly powerful."

I couldn't bear her writing even metaphorically that I might be able to penetrate her. Still, I was touched.

Mom, I thought, had always been far more able to penetrate me. I could not get her out of my system or out of, sad to say, my sex organs. (When she made me angry, sometimes my labia would throb, not pleasantly, but with a strong rhythm.) My defense of public, radical sexuality in the *Voice* always made me feel a bit weird, because it was my mother whose annoying, in-my-face sexuality had in fact ruined so many of my days.

And how could people think I was brave to write about my sex life, when my mother loved everything I said and did in the land of sex? Like the time, at the Thanksgiving table, when my mother had defended my right to have sex with multiple women, anonymously, in the back room of the Wonder Bar in the East Village!

I had written about those nights in a giant feature article in the *Voice*.

Although I hated it when Mom said anything about my sexuality, however positive—I thought of it as my sex effectively being in her mouth—I had in fact brought up my sex article myself as we all were munching turkey.

I had begun telling my whole extended family the story of the trouble that my sex-in-bars article had gotten me into at my feminist karate school, before realizing that I would have to specify what the article was about. I have to admit I enjoyed displaying before my family the specter of my finger-fucking anonymous women in the dark. Especially, sticking it in the face of my mother and my aunt, the avatars of in-your-face female sexuality in my family. My aunt Natalie was like my mother but more cloacal, constantly trying to embarrass us by making loud jokes about sucking cock, overly-large vaginas, and doody.

My sister Aphra, who's also gay, had looked at me sidelong with an astonished smile—had I found a way to be even more outré than Mom? Had I found a way to exhibit myself that could actually compete with the way my mother exhibited herself? And though my mom proudly endorsed my behavior at that 1991 Thanksgiving table, her voice quavered a little as she did so.

This was extremely gratifying.

But my victory, like all my victories in sex-land, was hollow. Something was always happening that made my mother the real transgressor again. Like the time my mother drove me to her house over the Brooklyn Bridge and suddenly misplacing her house keys on the car seat, in the middle of the bridge, searched madly among my upper thighs for them.

My thighs, in their skirt, were not hiding keys and did not have keys or key chains mysteriously sticking out of them. But my mother fondled and worried them as if they did.

"Be more careful when you're touching my thighs! " I suggested finally in a fierce whisper. We were still on the bridge, close to the Brooklyn off-ramp. The keys had already been found, in my mother's pocketbook.

My mother saw red. "You're calling me a sex pervert!" She continued shouting at me for an hour. "You're nothing but a piece of shit. Just a piece of shit!"

But a week later, my mom was calling me up to tell me that week's article was brilliant. (She used the word "brilliant." She always did, with me.) And to croon how much she loved me, making sounds like tiny kisses across the phone. "I love you so much."

I loved her tiny kisses. They were hot, and sweet, and sounded perfumed—oh, everything I wanted a mother's kisses to be.

How could I not want to suck up as much of that love as I could?

Overnight, I had become A Quantity at the *Voice*. My firsthand article about Republican delegates beating up ACT UP demonstrators at the 1988 Republican convention—my essay telling straight people why they should be brave already and support us—my how-to guide on lesbian safer sex (for I was sick of people thinking that dykes had no real body fluids) had transformed my social position from that of an emotionally crippled, fearful and awkward twenty-three-year-old to that of an emotionally crippled, passionate, enthusiastic, fearful and awkward twenty-three-year-old who was hailed as a good writer and had the power to change things in the world.

It was heady to call up officials and businesspeople and say, "This is Donna Minkowitz from the *Village Voice*." They usually made haste to give me what I wanted, or at least to attempt to mollify me with reports, data, statements on the record that I could use to make them look bad, and (I had had no idea!) free books, film and show tickets if they were publishers or producers.

Sometimes I actually changed things. My writing about the vicious anti-gay murder of a twenty-eight-year-old gay male prostitute in Queens, Julio Rivera, made the police and district attorney take the killing more seriously and actually arrest the white teenage killers, who had confessed to witnesses. (They were all convicted, except the one who fled the country.)

It wasn't just my writing that did it, of course. Not hardly. There was fierce and sustained activism from many people, including Julio's best friend, Alan, and a lightning-like activist named Matt Foreman, and a new group called Queer Nation, which included a few of my friends. But what power I did have startled me.

I could do stuff.

Before this case, New York police and D.A.s had almost entirely ignored anti-gay violence, even murders.

After this case: I was safer. So were others like me.

Also: I learned how to write. Richard the giant sea-monster taught me how to do a lot of it, surprising me by how much he was willing to give of himself as he showed me how to lay down snazzy beginnings, build emotion, use structure. Like many editors, he even gave me some actual sentences I could use in my pieces, filling them in like glue in the cracks where things needed to be fastened together, clarifying my more amorphous thoughts as though they had been filtered through silver. Making my punches harder.

So. I became rather a well-known writer in a number of New York circles, reader. Not all of them gay! Oh sweet reader, forgive the sharp, pointy chip on my shoulder as I must insist once again that the *Voice* was a good paper in those days, that people adored it and followed its writing and politics intently, that straight people read the gay and lesbian articles and Italian-Americans from Bay Ridge the black ones and seventy-year-old Korean women the queer S/M ones and South Bronx Puerto Rican teenagers the English poetry ones. Looked at objectively (oh reader, you're gonna think I am a narcissistic asshole!), the work I did was good and it made a difference.

People aren't supposed to say that. But I am not actually a person—maybe I can say it? I am praying as I write this memoir for many things, that it be pretty, reader, that it be real, that it send, as Samuel Goldwyn would say, the right sort of telegram. On the deepest level, little one, I want this memoir to be truthful, so I've reported this fact even though it's more than a bit painful now to say that my work made a difference, because my arms hurt too much now to ever be able to do that work again, because I am such a different person from the one who did that stuff so long ago, and because I'm afraid of people challenging it, making fun of me.

Let them mock me. I will mock myself! And do it first. But despite my heroic gay writing, I knew each day as I saved butch maidens and sweet fresh-faced gay boys that I was, in fact, a conjured assemblage of walking, rotting trash, the contents of a garbage can that had somehow been made to stand and do gay-rights reporting in the shape of a human being. The ancient pagan and Jewish spells that my mother had put on me did somewhat to mask my moldy-earth and rotten-egg odor, but I had been warned by several rabbinic

43

authorities I had consulted that anyone who was walking by and thought about the stench above my head for two seconds would get that it was coming from me.

Magical beings and golems did not have any civil or human rights protections in those days—we have even less now, after 9/11 and John Yoo—and I was fearful all the time, knowing I could be discovered and deported straight to Hell, the home of recalcitrant magical beings since Yaldabaoth (Yahweh's true, unsacramental name) first put us there.

Knowing what I was, and why—a charmed bit of shit attempting to lead a human life—it was hard to take myself seriously as anybody's human friend or lover or fellow worker or even acquaintance.

As an activist or a journalist, it was different. I had a *purpose*. But in the solely human and personal world of relationships with lively, warm, unmanufactured human beings, I knew I was a washout. So I hardly ever attempted them. Even though I wrote passionately on behalf of ACT UP—and I came to every meeting, ACT UP girls were far too sexy for me to imagine I might do anything with them. Too sexy and interesting and cool for me to even befriend.

Human lesbians in general were terrifying for me. Unless, perhaps, they were very unattractive. Even then, it was not easy. Gay boys were much easier, and my sweetest associations in ACT UP were with them, a nice talk on the way to a demonstration, a chat about the joys of rimming with Saran Wrap on the bus ride home. But even with them, my relationships did not grow to a dinner, a house visit. With my straight friends, there were dinners but little intimacy. There were drinks, but a lack of anything profound.

I did have a couple of dyke friends from feminist karate school—I somehow forced myself to be in that environment, so that I would have to relate at least part of the time to human lesbians. Our *Goju-ryu* school ("hard and soft," our karate style meant in Japanese) was at least 90 percent human dykes, most under the age of thirty. They frightened me because, dear reader, they might induce me by their voluptuous muscles and soul-stirring availability to have sex with them, and that was something, love, I was very scared to do.

CHAPTER 5

OK, late that year, after writing for the *Voice* for some eight months, I finally got up the courage and went out with a cute but acerbic dyke who'd noticed me in karate. Jen made the point of telling me, though, that I'd only been her second choice. Mean little Annabel didn't want her, Jen informed me, so I had the chance to date Jen even though I didn't quite rate.

Because I knew that a large part of me was composed of fecal matter that had been sung to with the dulcet melodies of Romania, I didn't mind. I felt lucky to be dating Jen at all. I had spent my entire time at Yale and the two years afterwards not having any sex at all.

I didn't know why I'd been alone during those six years— I'd really wanted to meet someone— but Kieran, my evil high-school girlfriend, had broken up with me right before freshman year and then gone with me anyhow to Yale. Then my father died. College had been sterile for me in every way, but especially in a physical one, so that I'd barely even noticed the buds on the trees in springtime or the tastes of foods. It was as though I'd never read the *Village Voice* at all. And for the first time, I'd drank to the point of being really drunk, often.

In high school my friends and I had drunken small amounts of wine while eating delicious voluptuous runny cheeses and fat juicy grapes, and celebrating Bacchus by declaiming aloud in ancient Greek and kissing one another. At

Yale, the home of boarding-school kids more practiced in the colder arts of invading liquor cabinets and getting into Upper East Side bars, there had been something called "neutron bomb parties"—this was during the Reagan presidency—where you were supposed to "destroy yourselves but leave the buildings intact." The buildings were historic and beautiful, after all.

Also at Yale, I stopped writing poetry. And, while I'd never been able to masturbate—it is unclear whether any golems could, but my mother had certainly built me with that capacity disabled—my furious efforts to try harder while at Yale had met with no success. It just never seemed to work. Sometimes, I just felt a little pain. No pleasure ever, except at the very beginning. Still, Yale was the first place where I had ever felt dry through and through. My mother made me inhuman but she did not make me inorganic, at least not mostly. (There were not many preservatives. In certain terrible situations I had to take care, like the Wicked Witch of the West, not to melt.) Yet there had always been water inside me, even if not a soul. "Swimmer in the desert/needs to do T'ai Chi," I would read from Olga Broumas in my room in Morse, the ugly, modern dorm that had uncanny angles in the floors, and icky, hexagonal gray stones all over, inside and out, like a building arranged for evil sorcery. "To keep/in shape by moonlight, airstroked/ spit shine on the lip. So dry inside/the landlocked boat to dreamlife."

I didn't know why I never had a date. I'd felt really sexy in high school. At Yale I did try. I got crushes on straight women and invited them to dinner in the Yale dining hall. What we ate—nut-and-cheese casserole, bone-dry flounder—was as boring as the company. The food at Yale was terrible except for Christmas Dinner, when men in Elizabethan costume would bring in a boar with an apple in its mouth and they would have black women in maids' uniforms serving spiked eggnog to us in the dorm library. I distinctly remember, over undersalted nut-and-cheese, reader, having a crush on one quite homely straight woman, Ellen, precisely because she was boring inside and out. (Sorry, Ellen!) I think her being boring made me feel comfortable with her; in my Yale days, boring seemed kind.

By senior year, I was doing better: I developed a crush on a beautiful bisexual woman named Annie but she was enjoying a wild affair with her Literary Theory T. A. and obviously didn't want me. I pursued her anyway. That summer, redheaded, fine boned Annie Phillips sent me postcards from the socialist dairy cooperative we were both supporting in Nicaragua —with tantalizingly mixed messages. But she never kissed me anywhere but the cheek.

Just wanting Annie and her small but muscular wrists and maddeningly sexy, light musky perfume was the most exciting thing I did in four years at Yale. Before then, my bone-dry equivalent of passion went into demonstrating against U.S. policy in Central America and dutifully organizing gay rights demonstrations and speakouts whose presumed benefits I could not enjoy. I went to every gay and lesbian dance at Yale—every single one in four years, about twenty dances—because I thought it was my duty; I had a terrible time, each time.

On some level I knew that I wouldn't meet anyone, and I didn't. I danced with unattractive women acquaintances—on purpose, because I was more comfortable around them—or with gay men. I danced sadly, flirting with no one, till the dance was over, around 1:00 a.m. Each time.

I would have superficially close friendships with gay men. I spilled my guts to Winston Finch IV until the end of freshman year, when I abruptly stopped speaking to him. As a junior, I told everything to Lawrence, a gay boy who came from the suburbs, then barely said hello to him by the end of senior year.

Once, I danced with a famous young gay male writer who was a member of my class, at one of our gay dances. The writer confided that he was terrified of women's breasts. I knew my breasts were no doubt jumping around while I was dancing, and I didn't know what to do.

I had in fact had sex with my high-school girlfriend, Kieran, but that had been—er—a complicated physical and mental endeavor for me. As I think first-time sex would necessarily have to have been for me, an imitation human being with a quite different chemical structure from the norm.

Reader, I am going to do something uncharacteristic here and throw a veil of shame up over my three years of sex with Kieran, because I don't know you well enough to discuss it yet. We will keep my embarrassing first attempts at accessing human physicality wrapped for now.

Karate, when I began to study it in 1986, was physical in a more profound way than the sex I had had so long ago with Kieran had been. Or, let us say that with karate I was able to master entering the world of flesh and blood, and interacting with it with my own clay and muffin batter, misshapen as it was. I had not been able to do this previously with sex.

I had never been a very physical child, because my mother had worked hardest at imitating the minds and thoughts of the humans, not their bodies. There had been no point in my doing sports, or even taking walks. Why should I attempt to feel like a human, or run about like a human, or even play like a human child, when the whole point was to entertain humans? Would a jack-in-the-box be designed so that it was able to run a four-minute mile?

I was an entertainment and connection golem, you must understand—not intended for defense except in the direst circumstances, like the very first golems that the rabbis had sent one another to demonstrate their prowess. My mother had taught me sleight of hand, but for us that involved Svengali skills more than hand-eye coordination, charm and deceptiveness more than any acute perception of spatial relations.

Organizing my limbs was indeed a trial for me as a child, because they and my trunk had been rather shoddily thrown together, if I may say so. (No offense, Mommy!) So if I moved my arms, my hips and belly would fling out like a rag doll. If I moved my neck, my head would bobble. But if I moved my head, my neck would seem to disappear.

It turned out that karate, which had been developed by people who saw past the flesh into the spirit, people who had been oppressed and did not have weapons, could be taught to anyone, human or golem, disabled person or triathlete or space alien.

It could be taught to women, and to slaves.

It could even be taught to me.

Years ago, my day camp counselor had laughed at me one day when I tried to jump rope with the human girls, which I only did because the counselor had earnestly urged me to. "I know you can do it, " she said. But I hadn't ever been able to jump rope; I was now nine. The counselor hadn't realized I was made of such cheap materials. When she figured it out, she laughed.

After she'd laughed, I fantasized about buying a gun and killing her.

My father had started punching me two years before this, and it had not helped my consciousness of my body and its extent and parts, and how to make those different parts work together.

People had always been pointing out my rag-doll aspect.

"Whenever you eat, you close your eyes," the other kids had informed me in fourth grade. I hadn't been aware. Perhaps I'd enjoyed my food a lot?

"Thank God you weren't born a boy," my best friend in high school, Andrea Lichtman, told me. "You'd be absolutely unbearable then! You're already so absent-minded and disconnected from reality."

One semester in 10th grade I even claimed to be taking an adult education course in "Slimnastics" at the Forest Hills

Jewish Center so I could get out of gym class. I filled out a school form and signed in the name of the instructor.

I didn't want to hear any negative comments about the way I related to my body. Then again, my mother had made all sorts of positive comments about my body, which had been enormously worse.

When I was eleven and bought myself a pair of long blue-and-white two-toned boots, she said "I love those boots, they make you look like a dominatrix." I'd never heard of a dominatrix before, so my mother was delighted to explain.

When I was twelve, my mother had smiled salaciously at my waist and hips, smirking, "You have a great figure." Her eyes and lips would look wet and gleaming as she said it. She smirked this every year at me, till I was thirty-six.

She laughed at Josie for sleeping with her bra on. When Josie was a young adult, my mom would roll up Josie's blouse and pretend to peek at her tits.

The last time that I slept in a bed with my mother was around 1983, when I was in college. I was visiting her in her tiny apartment in Brooklyn and we slept in the big bed together. Shortly after we retired to bed, she intertwined her legs with mine.

I had to battle with her body all night to keep her legs from around my hips and calves.

Did she forget that it was me in the bed? Was she only dreaming? But why has no one else I've ever slept platonically in a bed with—sisters, acquaintances, friends—ever intertwined their legs with mine, waking or sleeping? Did my mother want to copulate with me?

When I started karate, I was living with my mom in a different apartment before going off to grad school. I had my own bed—a couch that folded out in the living room. I had insisted that my mother put up a door to the room, which she kindly agreed to purchase for me at "The Door Store," a famous Brooklyn emporium. But when she brought it home, it turned out to be a little, incomplete, swinging saloon door, like the one through which the bad guy bangs in a Western. It did not lock.

I don't remember much from that first summer with karate except that I loved it. And that my mother kicked me in the shins when she erroneously thought, as I have explained, that I was going to hit her when I demonstrated my new moves. And that my sister Josie, now installed in an elite management program, laughed at me when I practiced for her.

"You look so funny," she said.

But I was off after only two months to life-killing graduate school upstate—an assay in even greater academic dryness than college had been, which I thought would establish me in a humanities professorship, a dream of my mother's. It was not till I had escaped back to New York City the following January that I immersed myself in martial arts thoroughly.

When I was doing karate, I felt a number of things I had never felt before. What I remember most: How upset I would be whenever anyone's punches actually connected with my head. (We had a rule in our school that punchers were supposed to stop their punches a few inches shy of their opponent's head. But sometimes everyone messed up and mistook the distance.)

Yet this wasn't a bad thing. Strangely, it felt good to feel upset when this happened. For the first time, I was able to actively feel, almost taste, my memory of being hit by my father. I had always known that it had happened, but it was a bare, dry memory, like a dim and wispy recollection of my grandfather's face.

Feeling that sudden profound sense of sadness and defeat whenever Jill accidentally punched me in the head—and Sara, and Ginnie, in their turns, and knowing clearly where that sadness came from, was like remembering his smack in the face for the first time.

I would have to bow myself off the karate floor so I

could attempt to calm myself. We students were allowed to leave the training floor if we were ever overwhelmed by uncontrollable emotion.

Karate, indeed, touched its finger over many different sites of passion in me, not just the grief and weeping caused by being hit. I think it touched these points of emotion in all of us who were first training that year in that little women's dojo in Brooklyn. There was the new ability to feel positive about being sweaty, the strange capacity we discovered in ourselves to develop muscles (still a new capacity for women; this was the '80s). The mysterious and dangerous power to strike others. The very shocking fact that we could defend ourselves.

I had grown up not knowing that punches could ever be blocked, or ducked. It was a sweet amazement to me to learn that they could; and also to learn that attackers large or small could be, and frequently were, dissuaded from continuing by resistance as minuscule as yelling, throwing things, or making a scene.

Karatekas had perfected the yell, and instilled in themselves the ability to run away with no embarrassment whatsoever. If we had to, we could punch and kick; if not, our tradition said, "the best defense was not to be there" for the blow.

Sex was another place that karate kept stroking in us, and indeed, as a 90 percent lesbian institution, we had winds of lust continually blowing through the school, from the great high windows blowing seed-pods in, to the trembling sweat on our twenty-something arms and the sweet strange perfume of women.

The winds of lust blew in, and also, slightly differently, the winds of beauty. For karate was not just very sexy, it was also beautiful in its own right. Our katas—the dance-like combinations of movements through which karate had traditionally been taught—were beautiful, far beyond the practical benefit of the self-defense strikes they taught. They

53

were the most beautiful movements I had ever done, or seen done.

Apparently, somehow, I looked attractive doing them, because first Jennifer and then several other girls in the dojo and the activist scene asked me out, and I did have sex with them, reader. The winds of lust blew in even for me, and I did feel them again, sweet reader—most memorably with a girl who picked me up on the bus to a march on Washington against the first Gulf War (1991), a very young woman named Georgia from Texas who was impossibly handsome, muscular, and roguish. Yet when I had sex, I could tell I was only capable of a dim, thin shadow of the humans' feelings. Doing the motions but with not much payoff, like a giant robot dildo. The dildo could have a sad sort of spasm that was like a washing machine going through a very feeble spin cycle. It didn't feel much.

And I still didn't even know really how my body looked. That I had a waist and curves for example, or a derriere. I didn't ever have a full length mirror until I was thirty-two or so—I had never had one growing up—and I had no idea that my body looked beautiful in a feminine way, or that my waist and hips curved nicely.

Despite her low-throated, fulsome praise about "my figure," I think my mother actually hated feminine bodies other than her own. One of the first things she ever said to me about the female body was her telling me gleefully, when I was four, how her own mother had once informed her, "Miscarriage is when you give birth to a cat. " Grandma Ruthie had supposedly told my mother this when my *mom* was little, and my grandma had just had a miscarriage.

There was a strange series—seemingly, an infinite series—of confusing and shocking and inappropriate remarks here. It was clear from my mother's tone that *she* hadn't understood the "miscarriage-cat" remark when she was a child, that she'd been shocked and frightened by it. But I surely didn't comprehend the remark any better, at four, myself. Still, if she had been frightened and shocked and disgusted as a child, *I* was to be frightened and disgusted now, by way of a sort of transferred revenge on the part of my mother. First of all, what was a "miscarriage"? I had to ask because I had, of course, never heard of one. And to me, the simple definition of miscarriage was upsetting, but not as upsetting as the image of a bloody, clawing, mewling cat coming out of a woman's vagina.

Curiously, Grandma Ruthie was the only adult female we ever got to see regularly other than my mother. (My aunt was still a teenager.) My mother seized the opportunity to make fun of her mother's body every chance she got. "Her breasts hang down all the way to her toes!" my mother chortled to me. I was about five. "I bet she could fold them up like a bed sheet if she wanted to!" I was completely uncomprehending of what this meant, although I knew that Mommy was making fun of Grandma's breasts. What did it mean for breasts to hang down all the way to your toes? I wasn't all that clear on what breasts did when they were in their normal, presumably un-hanging state.

But my mother really got merciless on the subject of Grandma's vagina. Ruthie must have been going through menopause at the time. "Her vagina is dry and her doctor told her to go get a vibrator for it!" she announced delightedly to me when I was six. Finally, I comprehended this a little better—my mother had succeeded in getting across to me that Grandma Ruthie's vagina had dried up because it was old. But what I comprehended most from the experience was my mother's ecstatic, cackling, scornful joy that her own mother's vagina was now dry.

I myself, as far as I knew, didn't have a woman's body. My golem body was styled with two imitation-X chromosomes, but it was in fact inert and sexless as a worker bee's, female only in some dust-dry way that could never be expressed. Why my mother had made me female despite hating and envying other women's bodies I do not know, except that she hated and feared men's bodies even more. She often told my father, as we kids were sitting at the table, how disgusting his body was, smelly and ugly. In a more jovial mood, she would often laugh with my sisters and me about how horrid and funny penises looked, "like turkey gizzards." I had never seen one, so I had no basis for comparison. It was my mother who was constantly naked in our household, never my father.

My mother frequently said she couldn't have been a good parent to a son. "I would have hated him too much to take care of him."

We have to backtrack here, reader: it's 5th grade.

Apropos of nothing, my mother starts telling us about the New Testament figure Salome, the daughter (or adoptive daughter) of King Herod, who demanded John the Baptist's head on a plate as the price for her sexy dance in front of her father(or adoptive father).

My mother's studying the Bible at Union Theological Seminary. She begins talking about Salome all the time, bringing her up even though it has nothing to do with anything. Mom adores Salome, though I never can tell why. It's probably the sexy dancing, which my mom imitates by dressing in jeweled belts and skirts that make you think of the dance of the seven veils in all those Middle East movies that have the babes with the palm fronds. "Don't I look like Salome?" she says.

If you don't know the story, Salome really does get the guy's shaggy head on a plate.

My mother also often references, for no apparent reason, a rather disgusting Old Testament story in which a young girl is put into the bed of the Jewish king, an old man, "to warm it up." She loves this story and seems pretty turned on by it; it makes her chuckle.

One day, my mother casually tells us that her older brother Stanley saw a movie one year and came home and wanted to tell her all about it. He said, "Do you want to see what they did in this movie? I'm going to show you right now." And he raped her.

I have no idea how old they were.

Reader, I've met Stanley a bunch of times, twice when we went to visit him in the mental hospital. He was big and tall and fat, with filthy grey-black hair.

His wife is a *shiksa* elf named Elwyn, a starving-thin blonde who looks terrified all the time. (Years from now, she will slit her own throat. No lie.)

My mind can't figure out what to do with this new knowledge. I grasped years ago that my pain can never be compared with my mother's, that it will always be as nothing in comparison with hers. And that was because she had cancer! After she came home from Sloan-Kettering, she taught me it was wrong for me to ever be angry, sad or depressed because she just shouldn't have to deal with those feelings from me. She had too much on her plate already. But as she often says, I'm selfish. I go on feeling these things anyway. How could I go on feeling them after this news, though!

I am an even worse person than I thought, to have made her feel bad at any time, because of anything. Any pain of mine really *doesn't* matter after this, ever.

After Stanley, another man raped my mother when she was a teenager, when her parents had put her in a home for incorrigible youth. The man was the incorrigible home's director.

Stanley the rapist eventually left my mother all his money when he died. She had given him a lot of money, too, when he was ill. In a way, they were always going to be closer than anyone else could be, she explained.

In later life, my mother liked to sing me an old song from Yiddish vaudeville that seemed to perfectly capture her feelings about herself, the genders and our own relationship.

In an old man's comic voice, with a Yiddish accent, she sang:

"I ... don't like men,

Women I don't like, too,
Do I like myself?
I don't, don't, don't
But I do, do, do like *you*!!! "

As for me, I had felt like her magic mirror for so long.
Like the sexless wooden mirror of the Witch that had kept
having to reply to her question, "Who's the fairest one of all?"
And having to answer with the same word, "You!"
always.

So it was that, even with the way karate made me
shimmer, I wound up having paltry relationships for a rather
long time, reader, seventeen years.

The problem in relating to a human being wasn't even
the sex.

When I connected to a person in a way that involved the
golem's arms and lips and head and pussy—well, OK, so
maybe the problem *was* about the sex, but that was not the
whole of it. It was about how the body of the golem connected
to my Self—there were so many ways that just having a
golem's body got in the way of my *having* a self at all.
Coming close to a real human person with my—the
golem's—body, with the golem's self, never worked. I was
afraid that like my golem ancestors in the 16th century, like
the sci-fi robots who become too smart, I would be violent
and uncontrollable. But on the other hand, I was afraid that the
human being I was with would always end up commanding
me—as indeed, is the correct and proper relationship between
humans and golems, between humans and "robots," which
word comes from the Czech for slave or drudge.

But, reader, I did not want to be commanded! Reader, I
have always desired with all my teeth, my mouth, my energy,
to escape my bounds, and to violate the golem's sacred
charter!

CHAPTER 6

My prolonged study of the history of golems has convinced me that, if I were ever going to create a golem, I would first make sure to provide it with a really good trainer. Some instruction and molding after the initial efforts by the magician, to prevent the golem from going bad, or getting too strong. I'd get someone like a dog whisperer, or a really talented dominatrix.

But the perfect golem whisperer, I now know, would be a *therapist*.

I had had terrific schooling in high school and college, of course, and even a little graduate school, but it was not education aimed specifically at me as a golem. Indeed, my mother had sent me to all those schools not as a way of warding off the inevitable golem violence, but because she was a great big snob about academics, and intent on making each of her creations able to get work as a college professor or better.

My secondary training as a golem came later—came, in fact, at this very moment in the story, reader—when I acquired my very own mental health practitioner. And I thought I had sought out the therapist of my own accord. I just wanted a little help with the few technical problems I have mentioned, problems in getting my mossy clay to work OK in relationships with humans. I had started therapy at the same time as karate. But it seemed to be doing the exact opposite of what karate did for me. Where karate made me hot and alive, therapy was making me squarer, more rectangular, less like a human, colder—

Oh fuck, reader, I can't pretend anymore not to care about this.—Sadness everywhere, so thick around my chest it makes me tight, makes me quiet.

I am embarrassed. I am ashamed. And I am sad.

Oh reader, how sticky, hot, and entangled, how putrid, and how sad this place is!

I started going to Edna's little house at the age of twenty-two. She was in her late forties then, with a homely, pleasant Jewish face and discordantly burning eyes.

My mother's own shrink, Jane, was the one who had supplied me with Edna's name and number, through my mother. Jane had pointed my sister Josie to *her* therapist, too. My mom, in her more triumphalist moments, claimed that Jane was "the boss of all the therapists," like the Mafia *capo di capos*, and that mine and Josie's therapists took orders from hers. I thought she was only kidding!

I'd always liked tall, deep-voiced, very lesbian Jane. She had been almost a member of my family from the time I was eight, when my mom had started seeing her at the Speech Institute, which had many free services for laryngectomees. I'd often accompany my mother to therapy and send for the whole hour in the waiting room outside Jane's office, reading a spattered copy of the *New Yorker* (the first and only time I ever saw it). It was fun. Sometimes my mother took me out of school early to get a drum lesson from Julian, another client of Jane's, while mom had her session. He was a laryngectomee, alcoholic musician who lived in a flophouse.

Soon, Jane went into private practice in a fancy white-brick apartment building in the Village, and my entire family would troop down from the Bronx each week to have dinner with my mom after her therapy, as though to support and honor my mother for sticking with the process. (Yes, we had moved to the Bronx for a little while, one of the eleven total apartments we lived in till I went to college.) Meeting my mom, we'd have spaghetti with meat sauce at the greasy spoon on Waverly, which was fun, too. We'd gawk at the insanely expensive, gorgeous food for sale at Balducci's, a paradisical food store the therapist had told my mom about. Jane shopped there. My mother later told me that Jane never made my mother pay any fee at all, even after she'd been in private practice for twenty years and my mom had made some money.

Jane seemed to make my mother calm. As a little girl, I deeply envied my mother for having her. My mom called her all the time, when she was scared, or upset, or just needed a friend. Jane seemed to be available all the time, like a pill. I would hear and see my mom calling her from her bedroom and from locations all over the city, weeping at pay phones; afterwards soft and blissful with relief. I wanted someone like that I could call, and had no one like that in my life.

So when I finally got a therapist of my own, I was expecting that she would be a kind of servant I could summon to relieve me of my own most difficult moods. I had studied ancient Greek and was fascinated to learn that therapist had originally meant *servant* or *henchman* in that language. A powerful servant to be sure, like an imprisoned genie. My mother had rubbed on the dusky lamp of her therapist often, and I had been in awe—I think my whole family had been in awe—of Jane's muscular, motherly, all-giving, obedient ability to take care of seemingly anything, even my mother's moods.

She gave Jane tasks that she did not want to accomplish herself. The year after I graduated college, like I mentioned, I lived in Brooklyn with my mother. I don't think I mentioned my mother's new boyfriend, Will, who was married and would conspicuously come over in the afternoons to have sex with her. When she'd come out of the bedroom, my mother's hair would be messy—one of the only times I ever saw it so— and her face hot and flushed.

I always felt confused when they came out, and had a seesaw sense of nausea when I'd see my mother's hastily rebuttoned clothing, her skin rosy underneath, looking damp.

Besides Will, there was also "the Con Ed guy"—what my mom and I always called him—a sexy, blue-eyed utility company repairman who'd become acquainted with my mom while fixing her wires, who always came over to have sex with my mom in his uniform. Mom told me about their assignations. The air seemed especially hot when he was there.

A year later, when I left grad school, I wanted to move back in with her on Kings Highway. My mother said mysteriously, "You can't, but I'm not going to tell you why!" She added brightly, "But if you call Jane, she'll be very happy to tell you the reason!"

She'd arranged with her therapist to relieve her of the unpleasant burden of explaining it to me.

I never called Jane. I was too embarrassed. But also, I wanted my mother to talk to me herself if she had something to say.

Two months after mom tipped me off that I should talk to Jane, I began therapy with the woman Jane referred me to, Edna.

A couple of months into our therapy, Edna suggested that all four of us meet in Jane's handsome Soho loft for a "joint session," where the therapists would stand behind me and my mother like Athena and Aphrodite coaching their favorite fighters in the Iliad (to draw on a metaphor by Erica Jong in *Fear of Flying*).

In the beginning, doll, the session made me happy. The two therapists encouraged me to give voice to all the things I'd ever been angry at my mother about, or confused about. It was a long list.

But in response, my mother didn't say anything, not a word.

After my final, speedy recitation, "And then sometimes

you said very sexual things to me and you walked around the house naked and it was very confusing and upsetting. And sometimes your legs and hands shook and I didn't know why," my mother continued to remain spookily silent.

Jane took over. "I think we can tell Donna now, can't we, Miriam," she said in her very deep voice, "that you were sometimes taking drugs during those years, isn't that right?"

That was news to me. I'd had a suspicion or two, but that was all. No hard facts.

My mom was silent.

Did she blink in acknowledgment?

Did she make some sign with her eyes to confirm what Jane had said in that oracular, male-God-in-a-Bible-movie voice?

Did she give a tiny nod, so quickly I thought I might have made it up?

My memory can't decide if I saw her face do anything. It was that fleeting.

So it was that Jane took responsibility for my mother's drug use, not my mom. My mom herself never acknowledged to me that she'd abused any substances.

I don't know why I expected her to. She'd never acknowledged trying to get her leg around me that weird night in her basement apartment, either. Once though, years later, on a family vacation in South Beach, my mother told Josie and me we were "disgusting, ungrateful, ugly bitches" for three days straight, then blamed it on the shot of Demerol an obliging local doc had given her. She also sneered to Josie, "You'll never get a man!" Thankfully she didn't try that shit with me, because she had no idea how anxious I was about the possibility that I would never get a woman. She also told strangers in our vicinity—waiters at the restaurant, people in the hotel elevator—how much she hated us and how much she wanted to fuck *them*. "It was the Demerol," she explained to us later, back in Brooklyn.

In any case, my mother said not a word about drugs in

Jane's big blonde-wood office-apartment. She didn't have to. The ubiquitous genie had fessed up for her.

Other times, my mother used Jane's name as a sort of magic incantation for getting what she wanted. When I was fifteen, my mother suddenly wanted to get a dog, although she mostly wouldn't be home to walk it. "I'm forty-four years old, Jane says I can have a dog if I want to!" We had never had a pet before this, and I was frightened of dogs. Josie was extremely allergic and had asthma. Consuelo, my mother's new cocker spaniel, never got house-trained, and, confined to our kitchen, made doody several times a day on the kitchen floor, which I would usually clean up.

In the end, my mom gave Consuelo back to the previous owners. "It's just not a very good dog," she said. "Too much trouble."

Then, when I was away at college, my mother acquired a large pet rat she had rescued from being killed after it had been put through a series of medical experiments in the labs at Brooklyn College, where she had scientific contacts. Yep, to fill in for me in the household my mom had got herself a pet lab rat. But the rat grew so large and strong that my mother became afraid that it would bust out of its cage.

She gave Zeno back to be euthanized by the techs.

I felt sorry for Zeno, because this was the exact same reason all the golems in history had been put to death as well.

Even my earliest forerunners had been killed, the ones the rabbis in the Dark Ages had made as a parlor trick, or (once), because the rabbis were very hungry: the famous Calf Golem, shaped like a heifer and roasted over the coals for two starving rabbi gullets.

(You can't make this stuff up! Look in the Talmud.)

The parlor golems, for their part, had been snuffed out simply because the trick was over, like extinguishing the candles when you leave a room.

When I first realized I was a golem, I wondered how long I had before my mother took me to the muddy riverbanks to undo me.

I knew exactly how she would do it, too: on some dreary pier in the East River, she'd make me lie flat on my back, so she could reach all the parts of me easily, then swiftly raise a paper towel and erase one letter on my forehead, changing the word *emet*, TRUTH, the sign of the living golem, into plain old *met*, DEAD.

Long before environmentalism, the same recipe in the Kabbalah for creating golems contained the recipe for destroying them. My mother was fluent in Hebrew, the basic language for golem creation and destruction; her *zeyde*, a sweet and doting man, had taught her that the kabbalist could assume the powers of God once he or she had become holy and learned enough.

Once the student had attained that level, merely writing one of the true names of God in God's own language would make nearly-human beings rise and fall out of the dust.

Golems do not have defenders of our own, of course, because we are supposed to be defenders ourselves. We do not have protectors; we *are* protectors. Growing up, I had never had any kind of guardian. So I was amazed when, as a child, I first saw Jane with my mom. She seemed a stern, kind sort of superhero, like the enormous and well-muscled Asian servant, with rings in his ears, who protected Little Orphan Annie. Punjab was his name, and he wore a turban; he was her bodyguard. Daddy Warbucks had sent the wise Punjab to take care of Annie because he himself was so often off on the mysterious business of fighting communism and fascism.

It is not Edna's fault, I know, that I expected her, too, to be like Punjab, and relieve me of every burden that might ever fall on me. That winter when I started with her, I thought I would be able to summon Edna whenever I wanted her.

At first I called her from the pay phone at my job, at the Columbia Law School library, several times a week (once or twice, several times a day). I thought it was going to be one of the fringe benefits of therapy that I could call her whenever I was anxious or even just not 100 percent.

Edna swiftly disabused me of that notion. "I'm not going to do therapy with you over the phone!" she said when she picked up. She sounded royally pissed off.

But Jane had always done it with my mother, or so it had always seemed. So I began my experience with Edna feeling deeply frustrated and envious.

I had to pay Edna, too. Every single time.

Edna, what is more, immediately became angry at me for pestering her, for acting the neurotic way I always did in my relationships, for continually talking back. It was only the beginning of a large and pungent anger she would develop for me over 12 years, an anger that would be epic and (it's terrible, reader, but I am fiercely attracted to angry women) attractive to me. I didn't know that therapists sometimes got mad at their clients. I'd certainly never heard of Jane getting angry with my mother. So when Edna, only a few weeks into our therapy, spat out over the phone, "Only call me when it's important!" I thought it must mean I was a particularly detestable client.

Edna would often say, "I feel very, very frustrated with you!" When she ditched me, twelve years later, she made it clear that it was because of my own particularly frustrating qualities— and how spitting angry they made her. "WHY DO YOU KEEP COMING?" she asked me in sudden fury that day, in the middle of the session. "Why do you come here?!"

"You know the answer to that," I said, alarmed and a little angered now myself. "Because it helps me."

"Because I think," she said, as though I hadn't spoken, "THAT WE SHOULD JUST END IT!"

But oh, reader—despite how much Edna must have wanted to damn my eyes, she also did some things with me that were motherly and magical. (Was that her intention? Is that how they entrap you?)

Once she asked me what I would do if I found a strange sobbing child in the street.

"I would hold it in my arms and comfort it."

"Then, oh, Donna, why can't you do that to yourself? You would do it for a child you don't even know. Do this for yourself, too, not just for other people!"

This, I know, went against state regulations for those who work professionally with golems. Advice to us in self-care is limited by law. So wherever you are, Edna, thank you!

Another time, when I was crying, Edna thrust a stuffed animal into my arms. I know this sounds hokey. I now suspect that it might be poor therapeutic technique. But oh, Edna, it made me feel so good! Did you want to ensnare me by giving me more than anyone else ever had?

Another time she bought me a special present, a little red stuffed dragon.

But there were many aspects to Edna's personal enthusiasm for me that seemed disturbingly parochial. Edna enjoyed the fact that I was famous at the time as the dashing young gay reporter at the *Village Voice*, and she read and commented on every article I wrote every week. Then she told me that the extremely renowned (even-by-straight-people!) lesbian author N. C. had been her client, and that this woman and me were her two favorite lesbian writers in the world. (Edna was also, of course, a lesbian. This was a lesbian therapy Mafia I was dealing with.)

"It's OK to tell you about N. C. because she said I could," Edna said.

She often dropped N. C.'s name in sessions, for what reason I could not tell.

But I developed a complex about N. C. ever afterwards. N. C. had also co-founded a lesbian S/M activist and social group I later attended—I had sadomasochistic leanings, it turned out, as does almost every golem—and I felt nearly out of control with my feelings of competitiveness for her, notwithstanding that she was a bestselling, brilliant author who had won the National Book Award and I was a twenty-four year-old reporter.

What had Edna done with N. C. in therapy? What had they discussed about N. C.'s sadomasochism, and how did it color Edna's views of those feelings and practices (decidedly *against*)? Would she have been less opposed to my sadomasochism if she had not encountered it in a much stronger form first with N. C.?

Did Edna love me as much she loved N. C.? Would she love me more if I won a big literary prize like her? And what would happen to me with Edna if I ever got less famous? "I love having famous clients I can tell people about," she'd pronounced to me.

When *RENT*, the hit musical about starving artists in the East Village, came out, Edna announced, "One of the big female stars of *RENT* is a client of mine, but I can't tell youwhich one!" Edna thought it was OK to let me know as long as she did not say the precise name. It was left to me to memorize all the names of the female actors and guess, because there were only two women in remotely "starring" positions, that either Idina Menzel or Daphne Ruben-Vega was the star golem of my therapist. (I still cannot see those poor women's names in print without flinching and seeing Edna's pasty face.)

Other times, she seemed to be operating out of a bad self-help book. In my first apartment of my own in New York, Edna had me put up sayings she had written in her own hand, on my refrigerator door. She'd had me come up with the slogans on the spot as things I could say to myself to bolster my faith in my creative work. One I coughed up but did not find very encouraging was "Sappho's poems were used to wrap fish in" (which they were, at least according to the classicists I read thirty years ago).

Edna wrote it down in exuberant purple pen on her own shabby notebook paper, curly edges on the side from where it was ripped. What were the other mottoes for my edification? I can't remember, but I guess they were things like "I am a good writer," or maybe "Lenin started out as a film reviewer."

In retrospect, it does sound rather moving to have had all those brave, shabby papers up on my filthy refrigerator door, urging me to believe various things. At the time I hated them, both their stupid look and their saccharine hopefulness. I found them embarrassing, especially when I had someone over. It took me four months to realize that it would be OK if I took them down, that Edna did not come to my apartment and she wouldn't even know if they were off the fridge.

If she had been able to see my fridge, I surely would have kept them up. Among the many magical notions I had of therapy was that Edna must know better than I about what was good for me, that my health and peace depended doing what she told me. I was twenty-two years old, and thought that someone had to be on top in any relationship. If Edna wasn't going to be my servant, she would have to be my master.

Another magical notion was that I was supposed to blurt out whatever came into my head in therapy at any given moment, no matter what boundaries it might cross or how potentially insulting it could be. I believed, reader, that I had no choice; that when I stepped into the therapist's office, I became like a Ouija board or a god's oracle, compelled to testify. The unconscious would speak with no guards and no boundaries up, and my therapist would tell me what it meant.

Despite or because of this I was always very qualmish about what in God's name I was supposed to say, how much detail I was supposed to go into, what on earth was important. Once I was nervously rattling on about the five pounds I wanted to lose—I was quite thin in my 20s, reader—when I even more skittishly informed her, "It's hard to talk to you sometimes about wanting to lose weight, because you're um, kind of bigger than me."

Edna did not say, "And how does it make you feel that, as you say, I'm kind of bigger than you?" She said, "That was a really nasty thing for you to say to me! I'm very angry at you!"

I had meant that I was afraid it would be hard for her

personally if I talked about my very small weight "problem," but by what I said I had in fact hurt her.

We never talked about either my or her weight after that, ever again.

Edna didn't seem to like the language that I used about sex, either. In my early 20s, I was self-consciously "radical" as a feminist and queer activist: *fuck* was the word I usually said. Edna would correct me: "You mean have sex or make love." She didn't seem to like my action of fucking around any better, although I had no idea why. I tried not to notice her disapproving looks, grunts and sighs.

Surprising things I said always upset her. Which was especially hard because, a month after I had begun therapy, Edna said, "Are you trying to put me to sleep? I think you're boring me deliberately." After that, I became even more nervous with her. I was desperate to keep Edna entertained, like a comic who has to keep performing for the same jaded, hostile crowd.

Perhaps that was why one day, just a few months into our work together, when Edna surprisingly laughed and muttered, "Are you trying to turn me on?" , all I could do was very bewilderedly say the thing I thought she wanted me to, "Uh... Uh ...Yes. "

I was telling her about a date. I'm not sure what words I used, what might have stimulated her, reader. I was not trying to turn her on, but she had asked the question so happily, smiled warmly. That was so rare that I wanted badly to come to common ground with her about something, anything.

Even if it meant saying something false. I did want her to like something I said.

I imagined, because I had understood from my college reading of psychoanalytically-influenced literary criticism that sexual feelings were usually hot and rife between therapists and clients, that "trying to turn her on" somehow meant a major advance in our therapy. I thought it meant the therapy was working. *Now* we were getting somewhere!

And I thought, coming to a place of greater closeness. So I just coughed, blinked and just said yes.

Years later, she told me that she found me "attractive."

Eventually, even peeing became an issue between us. I was always afraid to come up and use Edna's bathroom before our session, because she liked me to wait for her to summon me upstairs in her majestic Brooklyn Heights duplex at the exact moment when she was ready for me. So I had to either hold it in or cut into my expensive session time by dashing off to the bathroom while the meter was running. This agitation of mine made me afraid about all sorts of physical needs and adjustments during therapy, so once when I felt hot I took my sweater off quickly, trying to defuse my "trespass" by doing it as swiftly as possible.

Edna said immediately, "You did that so seductively! You look like you're performing a striptease for me."

I didn't know what to say to that. But I became afraid of taking off my sweater after that, every time.

Oh reader, we so seldom talked about my own dark golem longings, my own terrible, dusty thirst for love. I wanted to be married, binding my poor clay-pigeon heart forever to somebody's real one. But I thought no one would ever want to do that with me. (Or if I did marry, I knew I would choose one of the lacerating women that I usually fell in love with, and be lacerated by her forever.) On the more mundane level of sex, I chose people like the woman who used to make love to me as though she were drilling through granite. Perhaps she glimpsed on some level that I was really an inanimate object, but my clay was not really that hard.

Instead of talking about these things, Edna and I used to talk about how I could shine a nicer, warmer love on my mother, who was about Edna's age.

For the next three years, she tried to bring me and my mother closer. ("Why don't you just trust her, Donna?" she would grumble at me.) But I felt a mystically monstrous thing happening in our therapy around 1990, when the rough and

71

hairy hand of my mother's servant, Jane, intruded visibly into my own therapeutic process with Edna, like the fleeting glimpse of a werewolf.

It was Edna herself who nonchalantly revealed Jane's scraggly fingers on the scale. She said, "Jane told me you're not paying enough attention to your mother's illness. She had a serious meeting with me to say that your mom is very ill and you're not acknowledging that."

Jane told her? It turned out not only that my mother's therapist stayed in very regular contact with Edna, but that she was in fact her therapeutic supervisor, or according to a certain way of thinking, her boss.

Jane actually was "the boss of all the therapists," if by that you meant all the therapists in my mother's world: my therapist, my sister Josie's therapist, the shrinks my mother had found for her good friends Loretta and Bill. All the therapists answered to Jane, just as all their clients answered to my mother. Thus was the order of rule maintained, so that everyone in my mother's sphere remained in their ordained places and the unique powers of my mother were preserved.

As for my mother's powers, they had indeed mutated during her long illness, but not in the direction of decreasing. Instead, they had, if it is possible, metastasized. My mother had said that she was "very ill" with a variety of lung diseases ever since her cancer operation in 1971, but she had never gone to the hospital for them, and the diseases came to seem more and more like a source of alchemical power, rather than a detriment to my mother's body or mind. I believe the permanent hole in her neck served as a chakra for performing certain reverse or electro-negative operations in kabbalistic magic, from which she derived her powers.

Jane had told Edna that my mother was going to die soon, but I think she was deluded by her mistress, whom she was helping to focus as much public and private attention as possible on the hole. Meditating on holes is a well-known energy focus in so-called "black" magic, which gives the potencies of death-in-life to the practitioner.

Her neck-hole looked rotten in some lights, and it stayed there uncannily in her neck while she lived on; as though its decaying force somehow allowed her to prolong her life unnaturally, like a vampire. Like the Burning Bush, my mother had a permanent fatal wound in herself, but she was not consumed. It was like an ongoing fountain of death.

When Jane spoke to my shrink about my mother's "impending" death, I was furious that my mother's attendant had poked her calloused hand into what I had thought was my independent therapy with Edna. But I did not know whether or not to believe that my mother was dying. Because she might be, because Jane might be right and I did not want my creator to die without my having given her love, I changed my rebellious ways and began to see her much more often—about once a week —and I began to be as agreeable to her as possible in all things.

It was like my earliest days of golemhood, before I'd become a radical reporter.

Indeed, I had recently been fighting with my mother at whiles, and opting not to see her for long periods, but now I softened and called her or allowed her to call me once a day. Edna had convinced me that my maker was entitled to this by all the moral strictures that I knew.

My therapist was very, very pleased by this new change in me. As it turned out, I came to have my doubts about my mother's imminent departure over the years (my mother did not actually pass, if you want to come right down to it, until 2002). So I talked to Edna once, I think around 1993, about the possibility of breaking off contact with my mother, who over time seemed more and more to be poisoning my life. Edna just looked at me grimly on that occasion and said, "You and I both know you don't want to do that."

Suddenly, my throat got very tight and I "knew" in a strained way, somehow, that I didn't want to. It can be difficult for golems to resist a human command, or even a bare suggestion. Our minds are made in such a way that we interpret everything as commands: only the powerful harnessing of my ancient rage toward my mother, along with focused meditation, had allowed me to oppose her in the first place.

Now Edna was hinting—commanding, if you're asking how I perceived her words—that I give up this herculean effort. The suggestion was so seductive, reader: it felt tremendously desirable to just let it all go, to give in. Peace and love. Intercourse and harmony.

So I did. Now, finally, my mind would be on a correct foundation, that of boundaryless intimacy and integration with all living forms.

Edna trained me further. Not only was I to love my mother, I was to love all my enemies, as Jesus commanded (Edna and I were Jews, but both highly susceptible to the Jesus message, for some reason).

I was to love and be nice to every single person who tried to do me wrong—and this was the true golem-whispering, the kernel of all of Edna's teaching to me.

Christian-right homophobes? Homeless men who said they wanted to fuck me? I was to project myself into their heads and adopt their intentions as my own.

Edna got me, against my own will in the matter, to always give my mother the numbers where I could be reached on vacation. Later, I told her I was struggling with a request from my mom that I act as her "voice" and read all her poems aloud for her at her many poetry readings.

"Come on," Edna whispered. "Can't you just do it for her?"

I could. In fact, I did.

In the end, we crashed and burned, my golem whisperer and I. For some reason, Edna could not quite keep her control over me after my first book was published in 1998, and things began to come undone in every quadrant of my life, as though the golem-spell holding me together were starting to unravel after so many years.

This is how it happened, best beloved: I was about to turn thirty-five (just a couple of years after thirty-three, when hobbits have their "coming of age," but golems, as far as I know, have no official coming of age, because they are understood to remain the same age at death as at conception. In Hebrew, one of the original meanings of golem is *embryo*.) My book *Ferocious Romance* came out but did quite badly, my compassionate reader. That is to say, it got some wonderful reviews, and even an award, but few people bought it.

I had not expected this. In order to write the book, and also because the *Voice's* new editor had refused to provide me the regular salary with which *Voice* writers were sometimes rewarded after years of being listed on the masthead as "contributors," I had stopped writing for the *Voice*.

It had taken two and a half years for me to write the book, and in that time I had become less famous. Much less famous if you want to be precise, gentle reader, so that you have probably never heard of me, but if you lived in New York in the late '80s and early '90s and were an artist or an activist or queer, you likely would have. Charlie Rose put me on his show! Now, having lost public knowledge of my name, and losing still more oodles of potential recognition because no one wanted to read my book, I was trying with my last bit of energy to have a sexual relationship that was sexually satisfying. If I couldn't get people to read my book, I could at least have sex, right? A journalist I barely knew had set me up with one Warda Hueppenstech, who was not especially attractive or nice but who wanted to go out with me. Was I desperate? Reader, you be the judge: I canceled a late-in-the-game book reading in Boston to have our date, because Warda was going out of town for a month after that.

On our second date, Warda insisted that we see Todd Solondz's *Happiness* even though I told her I was really not in the mood for a movie about a generally nice man who sexually abuses children. "I don't think it's a great movie for me to see on date night." Warda insisted, and I gave in with my customary goodhearted golem goodwill. When we went back to her apartment, Warda and I started having sex, but I became upset and told her the movie had dovetailed uncomfortably with my training at home. Warda decided to plunge right ahead by speaking erotically to me about rape and sexual abuse and telling me how much she wanted to fuck me and take me over. She said she knew from reading my book how much I wanted to do whatever any of my partners wanted.

Reader, I told you that I was a golem: perhaps you'll understand then why I stayed in her apartment, allowed her to fuck me that way, and felt great pleasure along with a shivery sadness and sense of doom.

I didn't want to have a third date with her. Despite all the pleasure, I knew that Warda was a boor, perhaps the least sensitive person I had ever been with. She was too dangerous to entrust my feelings with. I told Edna that a few days later in therapy.

Edna was furious. "You're not giving Warda a chance!" She made it clear that she wanted me to go back for another date with Warda, more dates, a whole run of them! She said my expectations of women were too high.

I went back out there to Warda for a couple of shivery months. She fucked my sweet golem body and it felt wonderful physically and very, very terrible emotionally, so that my inner cavities resounded with a feeling of utter occupation, and bedevilment. And I knew I never again wanted to be that intimate physically with someone I couldn't trust.

Edna and I fought about it. She was convinced I wasn't opening myself enough, and it was that matter of argument that ultimately ended with Edna throwing me out of therapy.

CHAPTER 7

When Edna dumped me, reader, I felt abandoned like a motherless animal, but also curiously free. In short order, all the other spells in my life began to unravel, too: I dumped my best friend, Andy, the gay man I had always felt "married to" and who didn't shtup me or call me back.

I'd loved Andy, reader. Let me make that very clear. It is even as true as my name being Donna that Andy had loved me.

Reader, first I'm going to describe Andy the way he actually looked, and then the more appropriate way he looked in my dreams.

He wasn't handsome, conventionally or otherwise. Tall, thinnish but a little lumpy, blond but balding in his late 20s. His voice was beautiful, though—soft but profound, a strong tenor with its own sure timbre. His body was storky, but I loved it because I loved him.

Now, the way Andy looked in my imagination showed more clearly that he came from Faerie—for Andy was no more human than me.

His long blond hair shone in ringlets like that of a sweet young king of fairyland. His look was kind but perilous, the way all the fairest of that kingdom look. His face was eternally hopeful, also smooth. His face really was hopeful, reader, with lots of light in it, but I must have been seriously deluding myself about the smoothness, because in actual obtrusive memory Andy almost always had a darkish beard.

Perhaps the skin next to the beard was smooth; I liked to think of Andy as semi-virginal, young, and preternaturally feminine. In my mind, Andy was an eternally beardless youth, a *kouros* from Greek mythology, with lips as red as his cherry must have been. Certainly, Andy was a femme—the kind of man that I like best—but his femininity was tempered with a rising masculine energy in his dark brown eyes and driving chin, and in his tallness, I told myself, like a perfect yin-yang prince here to restore empathy and wholeness to the world.

Andy and I never had sex, but we told each other we loved each other all the time, fervently, as if we were 19th-century same-sex poets having a romantic friendship. We had long, weepy goodbyes at the entrance to the subway station, every time we got together—marveled at by homeless men who didn't know what to make of our ardor, or our sexless, goopy kisses.

I was so much closer to him than I had been to any lover.

As for him, Andy had once told me that he loved me so much that if I ever left him, "he would stalk me." (He didn't, reader—didn't stalk me when I left him, which actually left me not a little disappointed.)

The first time I wanted to be Andy's friend was when I saw him dancing on The Disco Bus, which was what the people riding on it called one of the three buses that the Gay and Lesbian Anti-Violence Project had chartered for a raucous, five-borough demonstration against physical attacks on gay people. It was an intense demo, stopping at five sites where someone had been hurt sometime in the past two years.

The Disco Bus was the most fun one, where a sweet boom box was playing the happiest and most body-oriented of disco tunes—"Funky Town" and "Ring My Bell," songs from fifteen years previous, to which Andy was dancing giddily at the front of the bus.

I had, most unfortunately, disliked disco during its heyday (when it was loved by the most conventional and homophobic kids in my high school).

But now, watching Andy dance in rapture to "Ring My Bell," I understood its beauty for the first time. "Ring my bell," Anita Ward sang, and she wasn't even a little bit ashamed. She wanted someone to ring her bell. Andy moved his long body to the song, announcing to everyone how much he badly wanted to have his own bell rung. He sang the lyrics along with Anita; I was transfixed. He seemed, there at the front of the bus, to be a one-person force for personal and sexual liberation. His dancing was flamboyantly feminine, and he didn't appear to be scared or bothered by this at all.

It was difficult for me, as you might imagine, reader, to put my body into dancing. Golems can't dance, or perhaps it's that we are sick of dancing because we have danced for other people too damn much. I was amazed that Andy, someone who had even more to lose by being feminine than I did, could so nakedly show all the people on The Disco Bus how excited he was to have things done to his body.

Reader, how much I loved his bravery! I think I wanted to *be* Andy.

The other reason I wanted to be friends with Andy was that Jen, the woman from karate I'd gone out with, talked about him constantly. Jen was the girl who'd said I'd only been her second choice; Jen, who had long since stopped letting me fuck her but was now a friend, now claimed that Andy was one of a special, radiant breed of gay men we had both been looking for, and trying to emulate, for most of our short lives. He had sex with hundreds of different men, she said, whenever he wanted to, different men all the time, and with no problems and no sort of sexual lack at any moment whatsoever.

I had been waiting to meet someone like him since puberty.

Oh, reader, I had never known the simple level of connection to and enjoyment of the body that the humans seemed to take for granted. I wanted to be as free as the humans were to command my own body, and to dance wildly in it. And I thought that Andy as a representative of this special breed of gay men was the freest of all, someone who could teach me to be free.

And make me, finally, holy.

("Huh?" you're saying. Gulp, this was a bit of a complex matter, reader. Somewhere I think I knew that connecting to my own body would actually be a holy thing. But there was another aspect to the overtones of godliness: I had always felt myself horribly lacking in the sacred joy of sexuality because I was unable to be as sexual as my mother wanted me to be, at every single moment that she wanted me to. I did not want to make erotic jokes with her or tell her how gorgeous her breasts were. I did not want to rejoice in her ass. I did not want to hear her say how bouncy and hot my teenage figure was in its tight jeans.)

Reader, I thought this was because I had no sense of humor. I thought this was because I was a prim and unfree prude. I thought this was because I was no fun at all.

So it was that my mother was a goddess of sex who I was always failing, always disappointing.

Becoming friends with a member of "the radiant breed" who had sex at all hours would finally make me worthy of my mom, I thought.

(In a smaller way, my ex Jen was a goddess of sex for me, too, because she was nonmonogamous and bisexual and often rather cruel to her partners.)

Part of me wanted to become close with Jennifer's sex-god gay man, and perhaps take him from her.

Reader, that is exactly what I did! Although by the time Andy and I had become close, taking him from her or even hanging out with sex gods had become irrelevant.

That is because, to my complete surprise, I had found something much, much better than that: his friendship.

Andy was not from Olympus, it turned out, but from Faerie, my own realm. He was, shockingly, like me.

Andy often took a long time to call me back, but he did call me back, and then we talked for hours. Despite his periodic withdrawing, I had never found anything so tender and comforting. We talked about everything—what it was like to be hit or coerced, or to be seduced by evil wizards when we were children. How much we wanted to be open and to love.

I'd never talked to anyone else the way I talked to him. In the six years we were friends I felt a hot warmth like brandy in my insides.

Andy, who'd been a child actor, got me to understand theater and what it was and what it could do. This was something I had never grasped, because golem theater is focused far too completely on the reactions of the audience. He suggested seriously that I take Martha Sewall's class in performing with masks. I think he recognized me, reader.

He utterly and completely loved my work. And he hated my enemies, and made fun of them. When a lesbo writer we both knew responded angrily to a letter to the editor I'd written criticizing her, he jumped to my defense. The writer— a very nice woman and a good writer, actually—had unfortunately said that lesbians tended to make more money than straight women. But after I wrote a furious screed complaining, Andy and his friend Pete had made endless fun of Lesbo Writer's defensive reply, exclaiming loudly in restaurants, whenever they saw her, "Well, if it isn't Little Miss Minkowitz! I have a thing or two to say to you!"

My friend brought me impromptu gifts, like a book of Oscar Wilde's fairy tales, a battered copy of Sade's *Justine*.

I called Andy my brother. I'd never had one, and men were so identified with The Other in my family that the idea of having a brother was like entering into a family relationship with a boa constrictor, or an amphibian.

But Andy would call me "dear one," and in keeping with the tradition of males expending themselves on behalf of the women in my family, he said he would die for me.

"Er, isn't that a bit morbid?"

"Wouldn't you die for me?" Andy looked at me a little balefully.

"I would fight for you," I told him, meaning I would risk death but not try to seek it out.

Does all this sound fake to you? Bear with me. Before all the peculiar things that happened at the end, I felt utterly known by him, reader.

It would be easy to underestimate what this friendship gave me. I could talk to Andy about my vulnerabilities, my deep embarrassments. That hadn't really happened before for me with anyone. I could actually talk honestly about my powerful ambivalence about sex and getting close to people. More important than that, even, Andy was the first person I could ever reveal my anger to and still figure out how to keep him as my friend.

Golems have always had a difficult time getting angry without destroying entire villages and tearing human beings limb from limb. It was a possibility in myself that frightened me to death. But Andy and I worked out how to tell each other we were angry. I had never trusted anyone before this enough either to share my anger peacefully with them, or to let them tell me about theirs.

Was this trust? We listened to each other. How far it went may be another story, as it was a first-time trusting experience for me and surely one of the first times for my brother Andy, too.

When he didn't call me back for long periods, I'd get angry, and tell him so. I would also keep calling, partly harassing and partly desperate, pleading. Eventually, less desperate because I had actually understood that he loved me, I was not so wounded by his absences. When I became less woundable, he called me more frequently. Later on, Andy introduced me to his younger brother, Barry, an actor and writer who had just moved to New York. Barry and I started to socialize sometimes, too.

A year later, when Andy and Barry had a mega-fight,

Andy announced in sharp tones, "I don't want you to see or talk to Barry ever again!"

I could picture his eyes smoldering through the phone. His voice was stern, and I took it as an incontravenible command: I was heartsick to receive one from Andy. My only real friend had never given me a command before. I expected Andy to treat me like a human, not a golem.

I responded the way I usually do to people's commands: by getting shocked and upset but paralyzing myself—as with a convenient neurotoxin that I carried in my bag, so I would not go out of control and burn down all the goyim.

I did tell my friend I was perturbed by his demand that I choose between him and his brother. "I feel like you're trying to control me," I said.

"What if I want to control you?" said Andy quietly.

This statement, reader, paralyzed me even more. On the one hand, I was so horrified that I could not respond, like an insect that has been rendered immobile (this time by a larger, predatory bug).

On the other hand—oh reader, will it appall you if I tell you I also found Andy's saying he wanted to control me sexy? I did. God help me, I found it as sexy and romantic and steadfast as his promise to stalk me. Reader, I *told* you I was a golem.

His demand that I let him control me in this instance dramatically altered our relationship for me. It's true it was only the one instance, but his demand, and my failure to resist it, turned Andy into one of the humans for me, one of the owners: someone who felt entitled to master me.

I still loved Andy, but it was now like all the other loves in my life, a dangerous one in which I felt, once again, like a slave.

Still, I loved him! So much! In the moonlight, we would discuss our mutual attraction to sadomasochism and the ways we had tried to have it inform our sexual practice. In the rose gardens that we found in Greenwich Village (they are there, reader!) we reviewed his psyche and my own with compassion and even something close to objectivity. Andy came out to L. A. just to put on a tuxedo and watch me get my Lambda Literary Award at a glitzy awards ceremony. After he'd moved back to St. Louis, Andy flew to New York to celebrate my book party with me, hand over a huge bouquet of flowers, and introduce me at my reading for the partygoers.

I'd always been jealous of the men that Andy slept with for a night, an afternoon, an hour, but happily he had never had a boyfriend in all of the six years I knew him. "You're really smart!" Edna had said to me about this. She said Andy and I were "brilliant" because we'd chosen to be emotionally intimate with each other, not a member of the same sex we really craved.

I was jealous of Andy's other best friend, Ned, because Andy had once had sex with him. I have no idea if Andy was jealous of my girlfriends; I kept from him my plan that he eventually become the (artificially inseminating) father of my children.

Finally, Andy and I had a consummation of sorts at Justine, "an S/M restaurant" in Chelsea. Justine was a place on 23rd Street where you could order the kind of luxurious food that people imagined the Marquis de Sade eating, such as foie gras, whole sides of beef, and a decadent dessert served in a large female chocolate shoe. (The restaurant was as real as you are, reader. Don't second-guess me!) Guests could also order spankings and whippings, if the recipient was willing. A staff of male and female dominants in leather was on hand to fulfill the special orders; tips were encouraged.

Andy's people the Fair Folk, nearly wiped out by the church, have a hard time navigating the vicissitudes of love without employing at least a little protective cruelty. Certainly we golems do. My friend and I had spoken to each other about our longings to hurt and humiliate the rulers probably ever since our first luncheon at Café Otto (Andy called and invited *Qme* to lunch, our first official socializing; I think he had

84

considered *Qme* a god of writing).

By the time we'd gone out to dinner at Justine, I'd "given up" S/M, reader, after a disastrous relationship with a very mean bottom. Besides that lady's meanness, I was flabbergasted to find a lack of fulfillment in me when I hit someone—when, that is, I'd finally indulged those cravings that all golems are bred with, fear, are driven mad by, feel with our whitest-hot nerve endings, and eventually are killed because of. It felt nice at first, it's true—I could make believe the bottom was my father or mother—but after a few weeks it had stopped being fun in any way. I kept wishing my girlfriend would kiss me or hug me, but all she wanted was for me to pound on her. Every blow felt dead to me eventually, like a corpse made of old pain and old anger. Over time, the deadness of presenting these corpses even to someone who really wanted them got to me.

Andy was another matter, however. I knew perfectly well that we still had those longings in common—we continued to talk about them all the time. I saw no reason not to make use of the opportunity the S/M restaurant offered for a singular communion with my honey.

(I really, really liked that he was feminine but a top. I knew that *I* was sometimes too soft and not nearly mean enough at all, but Andy was someone who could be fey and fanciful and still *make people pay*.)

As we pushed foie gras in our insolent red mouths with our fingers, watching the action over by the red damasked draperies, the cute gay waiter asked us curiously, "Are you a couple?"

I was thrilled that he asked, though I knew I couldn't say yes. "We're a couple of very good friends."

Andy wanted to make it sound even more distant. "We're a couple o' homos!" he smirked.

Both of us certainly had a lot of residual anger towards men. So we "graciously" sent a spanking by a female dom to a handsome straight man at a nearby table, whom we both

85

found deeply annoying and attractive. He was a young, blond investment banker-type, with a female date who we imagined he was pushing into S/M when she didn't want to go there. Our fantasy was he was planning to beat and humiliate her— just because men are skeevy. We sent *him* the spanking instead by the beautiful young dom, and he'd accepted, taking off his shirt as she directed him and standing at the whipping post in the center of the room so she could paddle him with a leather implement and her hand, hard, while all the other diners watched. She bared his backside to the room, too, and we watched it get red; finally she offered me a chance to hit him myself.

I'm not sure why I agreed. It felt terrible to even approach this man with the paddle. I hadn't expected to ever hit anyone's backside erotically again. After I did it—one blow—it felt as bad as I had imagined hitting someone again would feel.

But—oddly, I know—this yucky enactment felt like a beautiful communion with Andy anyhow, as though we'd touched each other— safely—through the medium of the handsome banker's backside.

When we went outside, Andy needed a cigarette. Afterwards, he brought me the copy of Sade's novel— tenderly inscribed, "kisses, Andy."

So, how could such a deeply-felt union ever be parted?

Oh, baby, the worst thing about not being actual persons is that speech does not come naturally to us. We creatures of magic may be radiant—well, not me of course because golems are lumpy, though I am at least sparkly—but speech comes to our tongues as entertainment or wheedling, not a medium in which to be understood, or, hearing it, to understand.

Pure-form golems, of course, could not speak at all, a sign of their inferiority to humans. (Although in some versions of this story, the most famous golem in history, the famous Golem of Prague—given the sham, human name of Joseph so he could blend in with the others—could in fact talk and even fall in love.)

Anyhoo, I was *not* a pure-form golem. My mother, as I've said, was too fancy for that and also too much of a Europhile and Hellenist (she had too little love for, and too little confidence in, our purely Jewish styles and traditions).

And so she mixed my wet clay with various stinking compounds produced by the alchemical process. With leftover scraps of meat like the ones medieval biologists had tried, in the old days, to "turn into" mice. Stapled it all to a few old transistors or some hulking, primitive computer chips. Like the elves, I was technically able to speak, but speech for me was too suffused with power for communication. All that held me together, after all, was some Hebrew and binary.

Andy and I were made of words, we almost *were* words, and we could only with difficulty and the most aching pain communicate by them. Like baby Moses after he did as God directed and put those burning coals inside his mouth.

Andy had tried various things—to act, to direct, to write grants for a feminist organization he believed in. (See, reader, he really *was* a yin-yang hero!) He was also a dilettante, and never tried anything for long. (My knight was supported by, among other things, a small family oil well.) But it is hard to make a go of it as an artist in New York even if you do have a family oil well—so he decided, shortly before my book came out, to relocate to his native St. Louis where it was easier to be an artist because rents were cheaper, and fewer people sneered.

I was dismayed, of course, that he had moved away; it gave the lie to my fiction that he was my husband. But Andy had gotten noticeably stranger that year, and in fact it was the first time in our friendship that I began to think of him as a little bit crazy. He said his New York massage therapist could heal him over the phone by uttering magic spells through the live phone lines to St. Louis. He said that his golden aura had just become able to be perceived by spirit beings who were tickled by its merry, rambunctious particles and tended to giggle as a result. When he came to see me in Manhattan at a Cosi Sandwich Bar, he insisted that I sit on a peculiar, throne-like chair because, he said, he was there to serve me and to meet all my needs.

Still—we had one more act of intercourse, as it were, that was an even truer consummation for me than our visit to Justine. Andy coughed up hundreds of dollars for plane fare to L. A. and a hotel room (a different room than my hotel room, of course) to watch me get my Lambda Literary Award in May. This was a very husband- or boyfriend-like thing to do, I thought, and I was beyond thrilled that Andy had decided to be my escort. This was like he was saying to the world that he was my partner, my prince, and with me in a gorgeous purple velvet dress and Andy in his tux, it was like we were getting married. True, I did have to endure his tricking at the ceremony with a sweet young writer named Tom Flagstaff. Actually, I had an easier time with his fucking Tom than I'd thought, even though I was annoyed that Tom got to share my limelight by coming out with us to the special dinner Andy was taking me to after the awards ceremony. The two of them were clearly headed back to Andy's room. In the morning, when Andy and I met for breakfast—for of course we stayed in the same beautiful and romantic, Spanish-colonial hotel— he told me more intimate details about his sex with Tom than he had ever spilled about sex with anyone before, letting me know, for the first time, about a certain body part of his that was very sensitive, and how he tended to squirm when the area was touched.

Despite my jealousy about Tom, I was really touched by the intimacy of Andy revealing his sexual details. For the first time, I shared with him some information about precisely which little segments of my own body were likely to be most keenly attentive. At the time, this was as good as intimacy got for me, sweet little reader; Andy and I, clothed, at the Spanish-colonial hotel, talking about our various engorgements.

And I was glad I was much less jealous about Tom Flagstaff than I would have been in years previous; I did not hate the very nice little Tom, and did not even hate Andy for fucking a man the same weekend he was supposed to be attending to me.

In fact, his eagerly coughing up those hundreds to join me in L.A. is what felt the most significant to me, I think, reader, as though I was the woman Erica Jong had in mind when she described the widespread cultural fantasy of men appearing just in time to gloriously rescue women with "sperm, soapsuds, silks and satins, and of course, money."

I think I figured that because he made the commitment to cough up that money that he must be my Prince.

I wasn't counting on—among other things—our mutual language problems.

From the very beginning, Andy and I had communicated in a weird pidgin, as we thought befit two friends who were a golem and an elf who'd long since been abducted from fairyland and hurt. For example, we came up with the word "cheese" to mean something that was a little bit like Bill Clinton, but it is not clear at all what we meant by this. The way we used it, "cheese" could mean anything—something unctuous in a good way or a bad one, something with no meaning at all or something pregnant with meaning. That is my take on what we meant by "cheese," anyway—something that meant everything and nothing, just like Bill.

The way we used "cheese" was typical of our so-called common language. Reader, I believed our pidgin was a token of intimacy, a way of expressing thoughts only the two of us could share. In fact, it was a way to obfuscate—putting things in our strange code helped make them *less* understandable to both of us, and therefore made communication much bless intimate and dangerous. We might have been chattering in gibberish for all we were communicating to each other.

But—two months after our joyous reunion in L.A., Andy

invited me to stay at his mother and father's house in St. Louis, where Andy was living until he found an apartment. We'd never spent a whole week together before; but I, and I think my baby, too, were suffused with warm love for each other from the thrill of our sexual discussion and our Lambda Award partnering, as though we were now ready to take the next step in our relationship.

He was going to show me his hometown, site of his sorry elfin boyhood. I'd met Andy's folks before, of course, but this was first time I was going to be a guest in their home. I would get to spend a week with my quasi-in-laws as well as with Andy! They were going to buy me many expensive meals; and Andy and I had also arranged to watch The Who's *Tommy* on DVD together, my friend's favorite movie, about a boy who was as deaf, dumb, and blind as we two were with each other.

(Andy's father, Midwestern and portly, disrupted my wedding cloud by sharing some gossipy remarks about Andy's romantic life. "I really thought he was gonna marry Ned," Mr. Lionheart whispered conspiratorially, "but I guess that's not in the cards. We'll have to find some other great boy for him!")

Andy had also decided to use this visit to help me improve my skills with the ladies. Reader, I've told you already about my problems in this area. Now I must inform you that Andrew Lionheart had always been a much, much better flirt than I was, with men, women, or children, animals or vegetables. (Minerals were beneath his notice.) We were always having to pause in the middle of an intense, personal discussion over dinner so that he could flirt with the waiter. When we were walking together, Andy and I would always stop in midsentence so he could look back or forward to scan the area for appropriate male faces.

My friend proposed that I go out with him one night to a St. Louis gay bar. Now, gay bars in New York scared me silly—because in our city lesbians and gay men had almost entirely separate bars, so if I wanted to go out I would have to contend with a 100 percent concentration of lesbians on the prowl, which was so alluring and terrifying that my golem body nearly fell apart. It was hard for me to speak to anyone, especially women I found attractive. But out of the city, especially in smaller urbs like St. Louis, gay men and women tended to congregate in the same bars, which was much less frightening because the women were diluted by the men.

So I said yes to Andy's bar run. I did not know that he was going to invite several cute St. Louis lesbians he had recently met so that, he thought, I could improve my abysmal stats with women, start a long-distance relationship or even take a few of them to bed! (Proving that I was, just a little bit, fun.) When Andy invited one woman in my presence, I told him afterwards that I would be more comfortable with the two of us going alone. My friend was unwilling to endure the social awkwardness of breaking his invitation to this woman or the other two he had invited: "What do you think they'll think of me?"

So I went. The ill-fated outing was scheduled for a few days later. Thankfully, only one of the babes Andy had procured for me showed up. I dutifully flirted with her for twenty minutes while Andy discreetly stepped away. She wasn't very enticing, also thankfully, reader. Because only one of the lesbians showed, the bar outing wasn't worse than death, but I still hated it. Andy had insisted on advising me on what to wear, and he forced me to abandon my regular shorts for the holey ones I wore only to sleep.

The next day, however, my friend wanted to find out why getting to know girls scared me so much. I did not want to talk about it right then. He pressed me further: why did I hate flirting with women? We'd talked about my mother and father for years, but never directly about why flirting scared me. I hadn't discussed it because I was afraid of talking about what I saw as my outstanding inabilities in that area, which came indeed from the fear of being a deficient sex-toy, an appalling romance-toy, an insufficiently-entertaining robot dildo for these women.

The fear was much too raw for me to want to talk about it with Andy then. So I said, diplomatically as I thought, in our pidgin, "That threatens to put me in a dark corner."

—Suddenly, Andy was on me. Not physically, thank God, but with his voice—he was yelling at me louder than I'd ever been yelled at in my life.

"You're saying that I'm threatening you?!"

"No, I was saying that *that*—what we were talking about—was threatening to put me in a dark corner."

"That means you're saying that *I'm* threatening to put you in a dark corner!" He was livid. "You're saying I'm a threat to you!"

"No," I said, "you just misunderstood me. I'm not accusing you of threatening me at all."

"But you did!" he said. "And you said that I'm threatening to put you *in a dark corner*, which is a really bad place to be!"

"No—" I said. "You misunderstood—"

"Now you're doing it again! When you say that someone misunderstood, you're saying that someone else did something wrong. You're making a judgment. You should say that *you* failed to express yourself correctly."

"I didn't say you did anything wrong. Nothing wrong at all. But it's just literally true—you misunderstood me."

"There! You're doing it again!"

"Look, let's get beyond this *misunderstood* question. Let's simply say that what you heard is not what I intended."

"But you said it! Can't you take responsibility for it? And you said that I was threatening to put you in a dark corner, which like I said is a *very very bad* place to be—"

So it went on, for three hours. I should say that our argument began in the car—I don't know where we'd been driving—and that Andy soon pulled over to a secluded, leafy parking lot so he could scream at me in earnest.

I was paralyzed, as usual when attacked. At intervals I did try to get through to my friend ("Come on, Andy—this is *Qme*. Don't you remember me?") but I got nowhere.

At one point he deserted me so he could stand alone in the leafy roadside greenery and commune more deeply with his anger, stranding me in the car for forty minutes. (Like most golems, I don't drive, of course, reader.)

Afterwards, Andy was openly contemptuous of me ("You don't deserve for me to talk to you.")

When we returned to Andy's suburban manse, we spent four more hours arguing, all of them within earshot of Andy's nice dad, a retired executive at Honeywell. Although we soon shut ourselves in a study so we could close the door, I was very embarrassed because I knew we were yelling so loud that he could hear us anyway.

Yes, yes, I was yelling, too. Something I may have kept from you, reader, is that I was indeed capable of screaming in a fierce way that people occasionally found frightening. My inbred golem capacity for violence manifested itself not in blows—not in blows, ever—but in a brutal and foul quality in how I talked to people when I myself felt profoundly threatened. At those (unpredictable) times, it would be as though I had channeled my two parents, and the battering edge of their voices had entered me.

I don't know if this is how I yelled at Andy then— perhaps I yelled more timorously, because I was frightened that Andy and I were over. Or maybe my fear made me yell louder.

In any case, by the next day I was already hiding my feelings. Both of us were polite and very distant as Andy took me to a special local fried-chicken joint, a petting zoo for steers, a puppet museum. It was quite clear that he was not going to explain his screaming or apologize. He was certainly not going to exculpate me from the absolutely hellish thing he thought I had done, call him a violator. For that was surely the reason for his persecution of me the previous day. Andy and I—he even more than me, I think—were terrified of someday being violators ourselves, as most of the golems had eventually become, and it was not surprising, perhaps, that Andy could be driven insane by his imaginative fear that someone had said he had become one.

I hid my fury and hurt and alarm from him until a few weeks after I got home, reader. I decided that I needed to so I could get back to New York without incurring higher airplane costs by breaking the requirements of a Saturday night stay, or having to pay for a hotel. It meant that I had to hang out and pretend to be friendly with Andy for three more days, but because of my mother, I was used to lying about how friendly I felt towards people.

I interacted with him like a hostage, till I got on that plane. Once I'd been home safely for three weeks, I did call my friend and tell him I'd been scared by his behavior.

Andy refused to talk about it. But being dumped by Edna the therapist—just a few months previous—had given me a profound new sense of freedom and possibility, because it was actually so much better to be without Edna than it had been to be with her. Apparently, I did not need to stay with people forever.

Reader, I divorced him (although I did it in an unfortunately golem-like way). I returned few of his calls and barely spoke to him until we arranged for a dinner *tête-a-tête* when Andy would next come into the city in October. I took him to a beautiful and overpriced allegedly "natural" restaurant, Friend of a Farmer, for a sweet coming-together that he did not know was his farewell dinner.

It was harvest time. And we had harvest-like food, squashes stuffed with meat, fulsome salads, bright-green artichoke lasagna. I was sweet to Andy, maybe the most loving I've ever been in my life, because I knew what I was giving up shortly. There were tears underneath my sweetness. "This has been so wonderful," he said at the end of the evening. "You've been so loving." And then I stopped speaking to him.

Andy—if you are reading this, please forgive me. I did not know any other way to do it. Of all the skills little golems are not provided with when they emerge for the first time from their dank riverbeds, perhaps the most sorely lacking are ways to extricate themselves from other people (and ways to truly join them.)

I'm very sorry. But I could not stay married to you, little elf friend.

After Andy, I believed that I had nothing left to lose. I thought that I was going straight to hell, where Edna and my mom had always told me I would wind up. Disobedient golems always end up there, along with superfluous children and toys that can't play well with others. I had always straightened up and flown right; now it was time to get curvy, and fly badly. Which was great! I didn't care that I would burn up, because I was ready to stop obeying.

That is when I got involved with Gemma, and my arms broke.

CHAPTER 8

My life is swirling. I can do anything I want because I no longer have anything. I'm having sex with someone's mom and my hands, arms, shoulders, back and neck are in pain all the time, not from the sex—that only causes pain to my clitoris and vagina—but because something has happened to the parts of me that write.

There is pain and unbearable delight everywhere. I don't have to be nice to anyone, or work to become healthier, more moral, stronger, better. I don't have to pretend to like anything other than the things I do. What happens when I let Gemma into my house, each time, is exactly, exactly, exactly what I've always wanted.

Blonde Gemma wears butch clothes, but she's like an even more feminine James Dean, soulful and sad and full of empathy. Yet she is more like an overt gay man than Jimmy Dean ever was, with a touch of evil mischief to her the way some gay men put on eye shadow, or paint their nails dark blue. She's just as crazy as Dean.

She slaps my clit hard, gazing down at me with great intensity. Then in joyful triumph. Then: tight power. She laughs. I feel love in her touch and even in her gaze. She's strange. "I'm so crazy about you. I want to torture you," she says.

Like I mentioned, Gemma is in an "open relationship" with the woman she is married to, and—can I say that the following relationship is open, too?—their four- and one-and-a-half-year-old daughters. The family "openness" to all sorts of behaviors does not extend to Gemma's being allowed to tell Partner Ann about our relationship, or my being allowed to touch her in public, come to the house, or make any sort of emotional claim. Gemma and Ann have an agreement to be "discreet," though they consider themselves revolutionaries because they fuck folk like me whenever they want to. "We model ourselves on European men," Gemma tells me. "Do what you want, but never say a word." Although she hasn't told the Partner, Ann knows anyway, Gemma whispers in my ear, two fingers deep inside me.

In my mind, Ann knows anyway because what we have in my bedroom is a burning sun enclosed in that tight space. Gemma says that I have a tight space.

I've never been with anyone married before. It violates my standards for acceptable lovers. But—I've always believed that I *should* fuck married people. I've thought I ought to fuck everyone, anyone, twenty-four hours a day, in all possible combinations, whether I'm horny or not. I've never, ever been the sexual madwoman my mother wanted me to be. Now life is mad, and I am a woman, finally, finally.

Gemma touches me like flame. I do feel loved.

Her touches are so soft and so fleeting that I do feel like I'm being tortured. There are very many of them, but they make me into starving, thirsty Tantalus bound just out of reach of the wet fruit tree. (Tantalus was the scariest image out of Greek mythology for me as a little girl, scarier than the guy who got his liver eaten every day.)—Until she turns and slaps me, which is comfort and a tense frustration all at once. She teases me, and provokes me, and bothers me for hours, but to me the perpetual inconclusive stimulation feels like love, feels like I'm being babied. As though a mother were someone who kept her baby up through the night, tickled it whenever it got sleepy. Pulled on its toes.

She's the first mother I have been with. When I suck on

her breast the first time, she asks snidely, "Are you trying to get milk from it?"

"I'd like that, actually," I say, forthright.

She hesitates, bemused. "So would I."

(She's not nursing anymore, but she was barely six months ago. If she gave milk now, she would torment me with begging for tiny tastes, wouldn't let me feed until I shrieked.)

I am snotty now when I go to see my real mother. It's amazing what can happen when you learn you can do what you want to. On the express bus home from my mother's "exclusive" senior enclave in Queens, where I have not censored my back talk, I write in my notebook things for Gemma. "You make my pussy feel alive."

My Repetitive Strain arm injury—that's what it's called—hasn't exactly happened yet. Or in retrospect, it's probably ripening, deep in my red tendons, glowing, but I don't know it yet. My pussy suddenly *Q is* alive though, inflamed just like my arms. I am in a bright and wicked zone where I eat luxury meals without feeling guilty, don't always return my family's phone calls, don't spend weeks wondering if I've hurt a stranger's feelings. I feel beautiful for the first time.

Gemma is the first woman I've been with, after some thirty others, who I was actually attracted to. I have steered clear of beautiful, sexy, even cute people all my life; they're frightening. In twenty years of dating life, I have dated only the homely. The only reason I said yes to coffee with Gemma in the first place is I thought she was unavailable. Up to this point, if I've seen someone sexy, I've turned and run the other way.

Even seeing one of them briefly makes me seethe with seduction and shame. It is ugly to want them, as ugly as I surely am standing next to them. Every sexy person sticks a knife in me, simply by existing. When I walk by them, I am wrong, criminal for wanting someone who could never reciprocate, and about to be punished for it.

Gemma is beautiful. That's the first thing I thought when she came up and introduced herself in the Park Slope Food Coop, where I was shopping for my tofu franks and organic buns. It turned out I'd met her on the street before with Ann and the babies and forgotten her. Partner Ann knows me slightly from the Queer Jews Happy in Struggle consortium; both Gemma and Ann are big fans of my writing.

"Why don't you and Ann come to my New Year's Eve party?" I said to Gemma in the Coop. I am a sucker for big fans, anytime, anyplace.

She said she and Ann were committed elsewhere, but that she would love to have coffee with me. I glowed with being liked. Now, I had no reason to fear Gemma at this point; she was partnered. And, she apparently wanted to drink a warm beverage with me, which diminished her sex appeal even further. Plus, Ann was hideous-looking and they had little kids, how sexy could Gemma be?

At the Community Bookstore and Cafe, her voice was high but quiet, rhythmic. She was a professor of history of science at Rutgers, with a focus on queer theory. I could immediately see that Gemma *was* sexy, of course, hauntingly so. Her butch blondeness was delicate and unusual, face and body. Though her lissome slenderness edged her slightly towards the feminine, she had quite hard muscles, too, and a pacific confidence. But despite her sexiness, she was *nice*, even sweet. She ordered tea, universal drink of unthreatening wusses, and we discussed the socialist dream—"the only problem with communism is I think I would be required to give up my beach house," Gemma said—and the problems with people's assumptions about the sexlessness of children.

I was nervous—it was hard to look at her she was so bright—but she very gratifyingly praised my book, and even asked me to autograph it.

I was aware that Gemma was cooler than me, too, and not just because of her looks. I knew from Ann's constant contributions to the Queer Jews Happy in Struggle e-list that

Gemma and she did S/M with the real kind of whips used on bulls, which was more than I had done even in my S/M days. And many lesbian twenty-year-olds of a certain class drooled over Gemma, because she was a hot, hot starlet of queer theory. But she emailed me the very next day after our coffee date, which made me feel absolutely attractive as a friend. Her subject line was innocuous, dorky even—"Tea and Tropes." I felt cooler than her, and therefore cooler than cool, a heady feeling.

Actually I was lucky she showed up right around then, because I needed friends. I had just dumped two more of them, besides Andy. I'd decided Edna had trained me to stay with people far too long, just like I'd stayed too long with her. I was almost sure that Gemma could be a great replacement for Andy—they were both blond. (I hadn't turned blonde yet myself, best beloved.) The fact that I couldn't have sex with either of them (despite really wanting to) seemed like a sign that Gemma was supposed to be my friend. She began emailing me every day, each day's email friendlier and more intimate.

Have you ever felt important and stupid at once, kind of like when you realize you can order something for lunch that costs more than most people in the world make in a month? And you go ahead and order that foie gras special, and it makes you feel terrific? It makes you feel utterly powerful for a moment.

Then you feel just as humiliated and pathetic as ever.

Or:

I have such different selves. One day I'm a gentle boy who only wants to set the place settings for dinner, one day a smarmy academic fighting hard to impress the grossest higher-ups. Some days I'm a feminist mom who's really angry about sexism, others a misogynist who just wants to fuck every woman she meets.

Gemma wrote with great courage about all kinds of unacceptable emotions, the kind most of us edit out of conversation. So I dropped acid under this ethereal purple sky in Lithuania with Sevia, we were sitting on the side of a mountain, and I wished so hard that I didn't have children. . I wished that for about two and a half hours. . Sevia looked a little like Charlize Theron, she was the Slovenian prostitutes' union leader? We ate roasted potatoes and looked at wildflowers. Then I went back to the hotel.

Or she said how great it was to beat people bloody in karate, which I had stopped practicing some years ago. Thank god there are rules. . The fabulous thing about karate is you can beat the shit out of people without the risk that you'll turn them into nothing, butcher's meat, you can pound them and still leave them alive and basically OK except they need a couple of gauze pads and a shot of coffee.

Me, I had been writing about unacceptable emotions for twelve years, my entire writing life. I had been known for it, in fact. But I had not been having them. Vindictiveness, insane vagina, envy, wanting to be smashed like an automobile on a heap—

I hadn't felt them in my body. After I'd left home, there was a point at which I had felt some baby anger at my mother, but I'd started therapy around then and Edna had chopped up the animal inside me that she and her Radical Psychiatry comrades called the "pig."

One of the many reasons I no longer had anything to lose was that I had left the *Village Voice.*

Reader, I was worse at office politics than an obsequious but untrained gorilla, and I thought my only path to greater achievement lay straight through a slavish devotion to Richard. I brought my mentor the best bananas to be had for money, every day. I thought that they, along with my writing skills, would be enough—an effective case of sympathetic magic. (If I bring him bananas, I will eventually get bananas!) No use wondering why I was his only protégé, or why no one else ever challenged me for that position.

I disdained relationships with everyone else, including the editor in chief. Well, not that I disdained talking to the editor exactly, but I was scared of him and I wanted to stay in my proper place: I thought the *Voice* was a feudal system and I should relate only to the lord right above me.

Like most slaves, when I finally got some access to the mighty, I made a terrible botch of it.

I had been asked out to lunch by the publisher! This fortuitous event occurred because I had written a *Voice* article criticizing the *Voice* for hosting a speech by the anti-abortion Democratic governor of Pennsylvania, Robert Casey. (At the *Voice*, rebellion was sometimes rewarded, which made it a rather confusing place to work.)

I'd also finally made myself talk to the editor in chief, putting on my best clothes for him and picking the nits out of my hair.

I got the editor in chief, Jon Larsen, to agree that I would be the next person appointed to the position of staff writer, my greatest desire. Unfortunately, Jon himself soon resigned. But not to worry—I and another feminist writer wrote a terrific position paper calling on the owners to appoint the feminist editor Karen Durbin to take his place.

Amazingly, they did appoint her, reader! (Well, she had already been a candidate.)

In the course of the transition I had my scheduled lunch with the ever-youthful publisher, a handsome undead shapeshifter named David Schneiderman, and Schneiderman agreed that he would ask Karen to consider making me a staff writer.

But baby doll, trusting a golem—myself—with delicate office negotiations is like expecting a donkey to sell your exquisite foods at the Union Square Greenmarket, or an ant, however committed, to develop the blueprints for your business complex in Bahrain.

Karen Durbin, though a feminist, had no desire whatever to make me a staff writer. But when she informed me of this fact, grinning broadly and chain-smoking into my face, I was foolish enough to bring up what I thought was Schneiderman's "promise" to me. Reader, golems are so bad at human relations—especially ones involving power—that I did not realize that Karen was not going to appoint me staff writer when she didn't want to, and that David Schneiderman was not going to twist her arm.

She grinned even more when she told me at our subsequent meeting—after she had investigated the matter with David—that David had only promised to tell Karen that I "wanted to be staff writer."

Karen Durbin, in her early 60s, had a satyr's smile as she blew her smoke in my face and sneered across the table at me, checking out my hips. "I see that you didn't write quite enough articles in the past six months to entitle you to keep your health insurance as of next month."

This was an utter surprise to me, and I wept.

"But don't worry, out of the goodness of my heart I'll let you keep on the health insurance rolls this one time. Hey, I have a great suggestion for you," Karen added. "Susan Brownmiller"—the famous feminist who had penned *Men, Women, and Rape*—"once wrote for the *Voice*. You might have a brighter career outside this paper, too!"

I had been writing for the *Voice* for almost eight years by that point, and was the paper's best-known queer voice, and the most I had ever gotten paid there was $14,000 a year plus health insurance.

As for Richard the sea-monster, he had suddenly begun doubting my veracity the previous spring, after seven years of being my mentor. The cause was an article about Gay Men's Health Crisis's attempt to crush a union drive. It was just like all my other articles in the *Voice*, indeed, like all the articles that had ever *been* in the *Voice*, reader—opinionated. I was furious that GMHC was trying to squash its union and that it claimed union workers would provide bad health care. But after my column was published, Richard's friends in the management suite of GMHC called him to complain about me.

"They say they made all these really good arguments against the union and you wouldn't quote them," Richard said.

I had quoted GMHC's leaders, but I guess I hadn't included the quotes they wanted. I'd reported what I considered the most telling ones, like "Members of 1199 might decide to make a decision that's not in the best interests of people with AIDS."

Richard no longer trusted me from then on. But I continued, deep down to my golem's clay-colored toes, to trust him. He instituted a new policy of making me call back the people on every article I wrote after that, to check my quotes with them. After seven years, it was humiliating.

After Karen suggested that I might have more fun outside the *Voice*, every other *Voice* staffer I spoke to offered me their condolences, as it were—about Richard. "He didn't go to bat for you. He never does."

I defended Richard. "He's just a middle manager!" At the time, Richard was the executive editor of the paper. "He doesn't have the power."

The other writers and editors said, "He does."

Richard and I had spent hours inside his long, dark, tunnelly, smelly office lair talking about our parents, sex with waterbus, and what it was like to be members of a fearsome inhuman minority. Sea-monsters smell a little like reptiles, reader, and golems—what do golems smell like? Like rotten eggs, all the rabbis had warned me, but I had never smelled myself and I wondered inside, faintly, if I might actually might smell a bit more appealing, like jasmine.

I didn't really mind Richard's smell, because I loved my teacher, reader. In my mind I sometimes thought of him as my "master," as in the one who shapes and fathers the apprentice. We'd probably spent twenty hours a week together working intensely, deep inside his lair, for the past eight years. It was airless down there, and I would sometimes feel a little high. I would wash Richard's scales with warm sea water as we edited and wrote and talked gay liberation strategy. He liked to share his most curious and unusual sexual fantasies with me, and occasionally wanted to hear my own (I was far happier sharing mine than hearing his). He discussed his relationship with his boyfriend, his daily mental and physical health, but was not interested in the equivalents from me. I would try not to stare at his crotch but, reader, my poor eyes were always drawn there, as if it were the heaviest magnet for power in creation. He was, as I have said, the most dominant personage I have ever met.

In addition to giving me my first adult work, Richard had enlisted me as his soldier in various internecine battles at the *Voice*. Against gay men who wanted to be independent of him (he would helpfully tell me whenever these writers said mean things about me, all surprisingly behind my back). Against the straight men of the "hard news" section, whom he found profoundly threatening. He claimed they were campaigning to restrict the *Voice's* coverage to political and economic news and keep all "soft" cultural, feminist and queer writing out of the paper forever. I was terrified by his claims, and joined a cabal with him against the newsmen.

I'd told Richard often that I considered him like a father to me. (He was so much better than my real father, who sadly had never taught me anything.) Richard seemed uncomfortable with my filial feelings for him. Perhaps not unrelated, he had always told me he had no power whatsoever at the *Voice* (just as, come to think of it, my father had no power in our family).

I need to say a word or two here, sweet reader, about my veracity at the alternative newspaper of record. I already told you that I came there with no dedication to the truth whatsoever, in fact trained by my mother to be a liar. There may even be some sentences in this book that are not strictly accurate in the plainest sense of the word, viz. the creation of golems and so forth. But reader, this is not a work of journalism, not unalloyed journalism at least; it is a hybrid creature, just like me. At the *Voice* in my first days I reported one thing I had only heard about from witnesses, not observed directly (I did not know the standards yet for journalistic truth). Worse, I mistakenly said that one source was on the record when he actually wasn't (the guy forgave me, eventually). Everything else, as far as I can remember, was quite true, first because I came to understand this was required, and then because I actually changed, sweet one, from working there. Richard himself, the forthright young fact-checkers, our lawyers, and my own conscience, which had developed so slowly in my golem brain, over time made me want to write the truth. Indeed, I developed a burning desire to communicate what was really going on, which I have never lost.

It was Richard who'd never believed that he had any power whatsoever, no matter how high he ascended at the *Voice*. It was he who stayed awake nights worrying about his straight male rivals threatening him from below, who told me himself that he had no authority even when he had attained the No. 2 slot at the paper. I knew I had authority and wanted to speak the truth to my own power for a change—and so I decided to do as Karen hinted and leave her *Village Voice*, and write a book, and thus begin my first attempt at breaking out of this golem body.

So, reader,
Pain is bursting in my arms and flowering in my shoulder blades. It's so alive in my wrists I don't know if I'll ever be free of it. I can't sit in any kind of chair, soft or hard. I go from a soft one to a hard one so I can exchange one kind of pain for another.

I don't understand. The faintest touch on the shoulder is intense now, like a touch from a god. I have always wanted fire now I feel it.

When it first happens I don't know what it means. I have

been going to a ditsy trio of physical therapists for some minor wrist pain for months, but I've had Repetitive Strain Injury in a mild form before and I know it's very, very easy to correct.

One day it suddenly hurts much more.

"Tsk," I mock-reprove Gemma in a whisper, when she's slapped my hands because they are inadvertently covering my vagina, which she's commanded me to touch. "My hands are sensitive." So she just hits my labia instead.

Gemma and I are just romantic friends at first. "I fall in love every six months," she writes me, "if by falling in love you mean it always makes me happy when I see them, and it makes me want to get naked." In my innocence, I fail to grasp that she actually does get naked with these people. I think she's just being admirably open about the longings people feel even in long-term, monogamous relationships.

I think Gemma and I each have a powerful platonic crush on the other. (They are so beautiful, my platonic crushes, and can go on for so long.)

So Gemma starts to drop hints, but cautiously: "Ann and I give each other weekends off sometimes. Ann uses hers to meditate."

The one with the weekend off doesn't have to tend to the kids, or to her partner either.

I don't get it.

But the changes have already begun inside me. It's not Gemma's doing, exactly, but I am wet with new movement, sticky with electricity. I've begun to notice things about myself that I never wanted to see before. Among them: that I am still a virgin in my most tender places, where it counts. There is a scared girl guarding my deepest self, standing at the gates with a knife and a bike helmet. Because of her ceaseless efforts, after sex over a period of twenty-one years, with twenty-eight women and two men, I have somehow remained untouched. I've been hermetic, boarded up. I remember when I lost my actual hymen—and the beautiful state I was in right before.

I was 15, and wanted the sacred to come all the way inside me.

It never did. The girl has always been too vigilant.

I tell Gemma how virginal I feel. How innocent inside. And finally, after all these years, how open.

You have the most beautiful way of exposing your life, she writes in email. *I love how vulnerable you make yourself.*

We go to the movies once I've realized, after weeks of hints so broad they do not get past even me, that Gemma wants me, and once I have decided—an extraordinary act of will—that I want her, too. Choosing to have sex with someone is a decision I have almost never made in my life. I've just gone with almost everyone who wanted me, before this.

So we go see the kiddie movie *James and the Giant Peach.* I flirt with Gemma by getting truly afraid in the scary parts.

But in the cheapo Ukrainian restaurant afterwards, she puts her leg against me crudely. I am, in some inchoate way, profoundly disappointed. I expected—I dunno, something that was more about being attracted to me personally. Her leg up against me makes me feel like an interchangeable female, someone groped by an old man in a movie house.

I'm also not really sure I want to date a married woman, even one who has an outside-partners clause. Sonny and Lisa, friends who've survived my post-Edna purge, are skeptical. But then, they're friends from Al-Anon, and pretty tight-ass and moralistic in the Al-Anon tradition. I utterly enjoy being skeptical about Gemma right along with them, but by the end of the week I want her again. Maybe the mere fact that I can be critical of her confirms me in the rippling power that I feel. It's part of this gorgeous sense I have that I can actually do what I want.

(Edna hates adultery and would be furious if she saw me.)

People say that they can actually feel life surging in their blood, and it is true, I feel it surging in mine! I've never thought I could do what I wanted until now. Yet I finally understand I'm going to have this power for the rest of my life.

I invite Gemma over, our first visit in private. I play her the song that reminds me of her, "Temptation Waits" by Garbage. "I'll tell you something, I am a wolf but I like to wear sheep's clothing," a woman sings to us slowly. Her voice is the sexiest voice I've ever heard (like red honey, this one). She continues: "I am a bonfire. I am a vampire." Gemma has already told me that all her life, she's identified with vampires. I've told her I have always identified with their victims. Surprisingly, our curious, mutual fantasy doesn't give me pause. I just love that she is a vampire.

By the time the singer gets to the last line ("When I'm not sure what I'm looking for. /When I'm not sure who I am,")—we've started touching. But—it is boring! Her limbs are golden; our ruddy genitals are unveiled. Both of us have flesh that is taut. But so what? It feels like we are cold, plastic sex devices each of us has found in a motel, wrapped in cellophane—a convenience, for business travelers. We are polite as we quickly move against each other, like carpoolers.

"So this is sex for the sake of sex," I think in a dull voice. "It's empty."

But in a week something else happens. Hearken, reader: I am built small and cannot take very much in the vagina. Either that or I just haven't been fucked enough. Gemma discovers these specs—when I ask her to put even less inside me than she already has—and she smiles suddenly, dangerously. "Then I'm not going to give you anything there at all."

She is refusing to come inside me with even the small amount I want, she means.

I'm surprised. She starts to touch me only lightly as a butterfly edges on the lip of a gladiolus, a minimalism of touch. An almost unhearable tune. I'm confused, on edge, what am I supposed to do now? A half-shudder from somewhere. Do I have a prayer of liking this?

It is not nice, and then it is irritating. Then it starts almost to scare me. It's not enough, yet it's too much. That's the problem—it turns me on too much. So that I end up needing, depending on her to come inside. "Please fuck me," I say and she doesn't. "Please, I really want you to." The tip of her index finger is, maddeningly, on the right side of my labia. It lifts off just barely. An edge of her thumb is lazy on the left side of my clit. My voice starts to get hoarse and childlike, I say "please" again.

She looks interested. She smiles, looking down as she slowly strokes me, and remarks, "I want you to say 'please' so many times that you get angry."

I say, "Please."

I say, "Please."

A certain rage rises in me, a deep fear inside, a storm. There is a rage in my cunt like from someone starving. I have read about starving children and how they'll snatch food from the others, even from the ill and the dying. There is nothing they care about more than that. Am I going to get what I need? Tears leak from my eyes as she makes me turn over and slips into my cunt from behind. I don't know how many fingers she has in me. But however many, they are so welcome that it is surprising I have ever not wanted this, have ever not wanted Gemma to put whatever she wants to put inside me. Whenever she wants to. That I have ever not needed to be fucked elementally, at all costs. If someone asked me to hurt a child or old person now or risk not getting fucked by Gemma, I think that I would hurt them.

She fulfills my needs, apparently.

No one else has.

I feel like some secret flower-maiden someone has locked in a closet, getting it, getting the bee to come. It's astonishing that you can get the bee to come.

For 24 hours a day, not just when she's with me, I'm in

heaven. That is not a figure of speech. I live with God.

Gemma doesn't let me make love to her at all after she's started fucking me this way. After the first time with her I'm not allowed to touch, or even see, her secret body. And I like it that way.

All I can ever even graze with my hands is her arm above me, her bright head clamping me to the wall.

But this is no problem. Not one. Not even a little problem, a tiny issue. Not a negligible one. Actually, not touching her is one of the best parts—because I love, love, love being the only one who's given to.

My mother always told me I was selfish. It is, apparently, absolutely true. But Gemma seems to take it as some sort of talent that I have. "You're *so* selfish," she repeats my word smiling, punishing me and praising for me for it all at once by stroking the very center of my clit, the unbearable flesh bit, again and again and again. "*So* selfish."

The thing is, I really, truly *am* selfish. I don't give to charity, never give to beggars. I have never in my life been tempted to sponsor a Third World child for nineteen cents a day. I *always* turn the page. Little Frida will never send me her thanks, with a picture of her in her now-clean, third-hand dress. When people ask me for publishing advice, I never give any. I don't want to lift up a budding writer who might in time compete with me. If I give contacts and helpful hints I might give away points I ought to keep for myself.

How can I give anything away, I who have so little?

When I was at the *Village Voice*, I never gave my interns tasks that could conceivably help them become professional writers. I just made each and every one of them rearrange my files.

G. stimulates me always, at every second, even when it becomes horrible, even when I've had way beyond what anyone would ever like. Paradise is nothing more than being fed like this, surely.

Maybe the third time we have gotten together Gemma gazes intensely at me on her way out the door and says, "I think you're becoming a threat to my family."

I'm surprised. But ecstatic. No one's ever thought I was important enough to be a threat before. Certainly not in my role as a lover. I beam, a bright patch of sun on my night hallway.

She frowns. "You think this is *good* news?"

Of course I do. In my understanding, a threat is always the best thing possible, the most exciting, most important. Threats are what (and who) I love.

If I am a threat to Gemma's family, she must love me.

Also: I hate families.

She looks at me strangely for a moment and says "I'm so crazy about you." And her voice is ragged. Then she throws me up against the door and kisses me.

The rest of my life has been eclipsed by having sex with Gemma. Nothing is of significance, really, except things that relate to our sexual interplay, mind to mind or in person. Our constant emails to each other burn—I can't sleep some nights because my brain is boiling over with new sentences to send her—but Gemma says our intercourse is literally mind to mind, too, that she can feel me throughout the day with her body, can tell what sensations I feel at every moment, senses all of my experiences as they happen.

Gemma is surprisingly mystical for a libertine. She also felt her babies singing to her in the womb, and will never be able to contemplate having an abortion. (Though she would go to the barricades for any other woman's right to do so.) Gemma believes in mysterious forces, things beyond human control. She is a rigorous historian who believes in voices from beyond the grave and stirrings in the blood that cannot be denied. I think that is why I love her.

I don't feel an out-of-body interface to Gemma but I believe her when she tells me it is there. She is certainly present in all I do, see, take in, think about. I do manage to work on a little writing in this time period that is not a love letter to her, but all of it might as well be. Being fucked by Gemma somehow floods me with creativity, which I cannot remember happening with anyone else. Words are tumbling out of me about pleasure and hatred and unbearable sensations, about paradise, about loathing God because the pleasure that he gives me is too much.

God is "like a tree that has somehow gotten inside me," I write, inside my cunt is what I mean, God is torturing me sexually by "touching me constantly every moment like a scratchy and unbearably soft knit sweater that cannot be removed." I like it. But I hate it. But I don't mean that I hate being touched by Gemma.

In my new writing I go so far as to claim that I have some unique talent for sex, as though I were a golem sculpted by some secret porno-rabbi, programmed only for sensation. I write—and very painfully, I increasingly am also feeling—that this "talent" is also a unique wound, and I am a walking 5-foot-2 vagina. I have no skin. Or I am all skin. What is outside is always, also, in.

What I am writing about—and some of what Gemma is doing to my pussy—is scary, but it also partakes of my new beauty, my beatification if you like. Like I said, this is the first time I have ever felt beautiful, and some of my beauty lies in my selfish need, my childish need, my uncontrollable ability to feel sex.

I have to give a speech at the Jewish Community Center about being a Jewish Lesbian Writer. So I write the kind of speech I've never given before, about how I have never felt particularly Jewish or lesbian. I identify much more, I say, as a sort of sexy, holy kid on a motorcycle. The kid may be male. He's an effeminate boy with long hair. I think he has pork remnants on his fingers. (Or perhaps in is just the smell of cunt.) He loves women but also loves being passed around by men. He has been at the back of my mind, with a couple other secret identities, forever. I also often feel, and tell the bewildered audience, like a 19th century English Romantic poet.

I expect God to strike me down for saying that I think I'm sexy. Or for "feeling" even a little bit like Keats or Shelley.

God does nothing, but the other two lesbian writers on the panel attack me. One of them is really mad that I said I was attracted to men, too.

I propose a "sexual food column" to an important magazine, in which I will cover, among other things, our "Oedipal" pleasure in milk fat (the root, I am convinced, of the orgasms women get from eating cheesecake), and the sadistic joy of eating the tiny endangered French bird called the ortolan, which you eat with a bag over your head (to capture all the bird's odors, I am not making this up), crunching it down feathers, bones, and all.

I feel free, in a way I've never felt before. And I rock.

Gemma sometimes cancels our dates. She doesn't show up the night of my Jewish Community Center speech, after telling me how good it will be to sit in the audience hearing me and then take me home and fuck me. The kid may rock, but I am bereft.

Next she calls suddenly to cancel because it is time for her shift at the food coop. I go out to the park to deal with all the energy I suddenly have in my body; I have to shake and roll, all over the snow hills. When I get back, there's another message from Gemma, calling from the Cheese Department just to try and reach me in person, to connect. I can't forgive myself for having missed her call, but it is also romantic to have been stood up on a 0-degree day in the snow.

Next time she comes to my house Gemma says, "You're in a bad position. I have all the cards. You have none."

I am dumbfounded.

"I have all the power," she announces. "I don't blame

you at all if you think you have a raw deal." I do not have a raw deal. Not at all. Or if I have one, it's like Zeus's lover who gets to see him in his fatal glory, having a raw deal.

I reply, a bit angrily, that she's wrong. Gemma doesn't have all the power. I'm actually right, kind of. In sex she does nothing to me that I don't want. I could be the original *Cosmo* girl, the archetypal fully-choosing-and-consenting Virginia Slims woman. In fact, I can trust Gemma more in bed than any partner before. The one time she even uses *language* I don't want—"Be a good girl, just like your mother wants you to be"—she backtracks immediately when I say no. (The only time I do.) "No, no, forget that ... Uh, just like *QI* want you to be."

She is eager to please, in her way.

And she thinks I'm brilliant. I'm not kidding. My writing knocks Gemma's socks off.

Right off her feet!

There's something else. Whenever she fucks me she tells me I am "sweet and innocent." And "good." It is a fetish, sure. But it is also true.

I am pretty when I see her, not sluttish. One evening I am wearing a sleeveless top of white lace and a maroon velvet skirt, not too short. I could go to a party with important funders, in this outfit. "You look so nice," she says. "And I am so sloppy, tonight."

Gemma could never really be sloppy. She's too good-looking for that. But she is wearing undistinguished clothes. Gemma can never have worn sweatpants, but in my memory she is wearing something that might be a cross between sweatpants and black jeans. Perhaps they are old karate pants.

She is her unvarnished self, and I am freshly showered and talced.

She pushes me in the bedroom, lifts my skirt. I want desperately for her to touch my breasts, which she hardly ever does. But I want her to get what she wants, not me to get what I want. I don't care what I want. Gemma always turns me into a girl. A very sweet, young girl. "Can I take this off?" I whisper, about my top.

"No," she says, pleased. "I like you imprisoned in lace." I am frustrated so badly I can't see straight. But I'm so turned on.

I like to be imprisoned. By her. Even her partnership with Ann feels like a chain around my arms and legs, my mouth, my middle that allows me to be free.

One night I have my period but Gemma doesn't realize until she is about to leave. There is blood all over the pants that she must wear going home to Ann. Gemma laughs ruefully and wears the pants turned inside out. "I'm hoping she won't notice."

But there are other signs of me, apparently, on my lover. Gemma tells me Ann has warned her, "You're not being very discreet about Donna," even though Gemma has lied repeatedly and claimed that we are only friends. "This is the first time I've ever lied to her," Gemma says somberly. She strokes my hair. "I've lied!" They are allowed to fuck, but supposed to keep it under wraps enough that the other one doesn't notice. When asked directly, though, they are supposed to be honest. Secretly, I am so glad the Gemma feels the need to dissemble, that Ann can't help but be aware of me. And I'm openly delighted that my lover must go home to Ann with my blood all over her.

I collect the signs of me on Gemma, too. One sign is Gemma get extremely emotional during sex with me. "Do you realize that I'm coming, just from this?" and she sounds like she is crying. "Do you realize that I come from touching you?"

And she looks at me sometimes like I am a pool she wants to lap forever.

Perhaps because of this, it takes me a while to realize that their marriage is not as open as I think it is. I imagine our affair has the potential to grow into a lifelong passionate relationship, that Ann and Gemma and I and the children will spend tasteful but wild Christmases together at our Transylvanian-modeled mountain chalet, roasting free-range turkeys in an ecstatic kitchen lined in wine-dark velvet. We could be from a romance novel called Three-way Sweet Storm.

I have the capacity, perhaps because of the holy kid on a motorcycle, not to notice anything I do not want to notice. The kid has an extraordinary power to focus on one thing, like a woman's wet vaginal love for him, to the exclusion of all others. Like him, I have an enormous ability not to be aware. Perhaps I am in a trance state half the time.

Say that I'm drugged by the world, and have an addict's parched-mouthed need to get high on anything beautiful. So when Gemma mentions her and Ann's discretion-contract the third or so time we have sex, I don't say that I hate it. That I didn't expect it. (Why didn't I expect it?) That I was imagining the chalet in the mountains. But I try not to notice that she told me. I don't notice anything she does that troubles me, or might demean me in some way, or hurts.

Our chain itself, though, is exciting, and the ambiguity of our situation is what drew me in the first place. Nothing is sexier to me. Tenderly touching me Gemma says, "The only two things I'm serious about are sex and family," and the devastating ambiguity of that statement kills me. "Sex" and "family" are supposedly equal in that statement, but absolutely separate. Her refusal to acknowledge sexual love, refusal to acknowledge the mere fact that sometimes sex makes people feel things about each other, makes them want to be "family" to each other, is what, I think, excites me, brings me home to her, wins my heart forever.

One night she cancels because it is the only time the lawyer can meet with her and Ann to sign their second-parent adoption agreement. Soon after, she cancels the weekend I'm supposed to spend alone with her at their beach house. "I'm afraid of spending a whole weekend with you," she says. "I don't know what would happen then."

Another night Gemma surprises me with an expansion of our time allotment that is, surprisingly, just as unwelcome. Ann has unexpectedly jitneyed off to the beach house with the kids, leaving us with the entire evening and the humongous house on Carroll Street. Gemma wants to meet me for northern Italian food and then sleep in a bed with me, something we've never done. It makes me cross. Now Gemma wants to eat yuppie restaurant food with me, like an ordinary lover? I've wanted to for months. But we don't do things like ordinary lovers, as she's already warned me many times. The saving grace is what we do together isn't ordinary.

We don't have time to go to dinner ever, only to fuck. But every time we have a date, I take hours beforehand to prepare myself. Not just physically, but mentally. I ready myself for her. Perhaps I make myself innocent again, each time, so she can dirty me anew. Gemma and I are a myth together, like Penelope's shroud ripped up every night. My purity is magical. Every morning, like Scheherazade, I am still alive.

Gemma can't figure out why I'm mad about the suggestion to go out to dinner. I just know, sulkingly, that I must stick to the ritual of preparing myself at home. I scarf a dry peanut butter sandwich—all that young girls like me, the fantasizer inside me feels, should have—and go to Gemma's house for the first time. As soon as I open the beautiful black cast-iron gates, all my magic is undone. The Carroll Street brownstone is a gorgeous place, a massive bricolage of art and feminism and money that Gemma and Ann have pieced together from Victorian wood walls and leather sofas, radical paintings by now-famous Germans, peonies on most surfaces. On the windowsills are pink vagina sculptures Gemma's little girls have made. They are all modeled on Gemma's own, she tells me. All I can make out are big pink folds. In the mommies' bedroom, shockingly, Gemma weeps. "I've never had someone else in our bed before." But she hates monogamy. She fucks people in the people's beds all the time! Ann apparently does it, too! I can't tell whether to be moved that Gemma cares about dishonoring Ann's marriage bed, or furious. I feel rather weepy myself. As Gemma strokes me desultorily on the bed, all I want to do is go home and have hot cocoa and cookies.

Instead, we repair to my apartment. On my bachelor bed, Gemma talks about my vagina in the third person: "She's so tight and sweet. She's so sweet and innocent."

I like the words—I want to be tight for her, so she can feel her aggression stretching me forever. But for the first time since we've really done it, the sex doesn't work.

I don't care that it didn't work. I love what she said, remembering it the next day. I love her talking about my vagina as though it were more of a person than me.

"It's your body I miss," she emails, "not your mind." She tells me that in person, too. My body is, appropriately enough for Gemma and me, a properly desirable subordinate girl's body, slim, curvy, and firm enough to satisfy all the rules for how a slave-girl ought to look.

Theoretically, her wanting only my body should turn me on, but it doesn't. Good girls, after all, have good minds, too. I want her to savor and torment both. I tell myself that she does, too, like my mind. She's just having fun with me. After all, she was a big fan of my book. When I tell her, in person, that my mind's attached to my body she says, "C'mon, please," and smiles at me. "Let me objectify you."

On the early morning of our next date Gemma calls to cancel, on a cell phone I didn't know she had. She can't see me tonight because she has realized, horribly, going out the door, that "there are no green vegetables in the house." She can't fuck me, basically, because her children aren't getting enough nutrients.

"I haven't gotten broccoli." She sounds emotional about this, in a ditsy way. "My children need to have vegetables."

I don't mention that there are excellent mustard greens, kale, and broccoli at the twenty-four-hour Korean market across the street from my house.

"You're playing out something about them," I say, "with me." "Them" is what Gemma always calls her family when she plans our trysts. "They" won't be there. I won't have to be with "them." She talks about the other three as though they were extraterrestrials she found herself living with, whom she couldn't understand and who were quite possibly poisoning her kitchen.

Gemma is furious at the phrase *playing out.* "Don't psychoanalyze me!" Then she says piously, "I've been neglecting my family. And many times lately with Ann, I haven't been able to be fully present when I'm with her, because I was thinking about you."

I don't know how to begin to answer that one.

Gemma tries to make me understand. "I can't justify doing stuff that's just for myself this month. I will anyway, I need to, but—" Sex with me is just for her, I discover; it is like those small but rich desserts, marketed especially for women to consume alone.

It is strange to be competing with little girls for nutrients.

Then again, it's what I've been doing all my life. I've never stopped competing with the non-golem children, with all the other little souls throughout the world, with my sisters and my father, for good nutrients.

It's truly odd, though, to realize that Gemma wouldn't dream of doing anything "for me" in common parlance—that is to say, on my behalf, or because of some allegiance to me, or for the primary purpose of fulfilling my needs. When she touches me, when she calls me, she's not thinking of my needs at all. She's doing it for her.

It is one thing to be teased. It's quite another not to be given anything, for real.

So I break up with her.

I've broken up with a girlfriend once before, but she wasn't someone I had really wanted. This feels like the first time to me.

CHAPTER 9

I told Gemma that I wanted to break up but that I wanted one more date with her before we did. So we had one. It was ceremonious—she brought red wine, Gemma wore a dazzling white man's dress shirt and black pants for me, it was our best fucking ever. She hoisted my legs and arms around her and carried me into the bedroom like she was carrying me over a threshold. (Or like someone ferrying a sleepy child into bed.)

Two days earlier, my arms had become weird. I'd had my regular physical therapy that morning for a minor wrist problem that I'd had on and off for years, like I mentioned to you, honeybuns, nothing terrible. The specialist for this problemette, who was called a physiatrist, had sent me to a trio of phenomenally beautiful physical therapists. Now, physical therapists—I don't know whether you know this, reader—are often uncommonly beautiful physical specimens who rather resemble—this is really true—goddesses. Like goddesses in the sexist classical tradition, some of them have no ethics in them.

That morning, the PTs were planning something new for me. The three gorgeous ones gave me a test that involved squeezing a series of heavy metal grips, then lifting some strange weights that looked like little hockey pucks. "This hurts," I protested. But the young blonde therapist said: "We're measuring strength, pain doesn't matter in this test."

I said, "I don't think I should take this test." The brunette made a tiny smile and said, "Everybody has to." It was a policy of the Zwieback Rehabilitation Institute that everybody had to be tested at regular intervals, for Zwieback's prestigious large-data study. The jet-black haired one just looked me in the eye and said, "Squeeze."

I squeezed. And there and then, in the twinkling of an eye, in Zwieback's odd, white, plastic-Lego-looking complex in East South midtown, began something different, reader, than I'd ever known—at least directly, responsibly, consciously. A world of immediate pain and terror, irremediable, sharp, frumpy—sharp points not just at my wrists but going all the way through me, a cutting and smashing and burning I did not think I would ever be rid of.

What did I have? (What do I have, I should say, for certainly I have it still.) My problem is called Repetitive Strain Injury, which is a "musculoskeletal condition" people get from infelicitous repetitive endeavors of all kinds. Assembly-line workers, musicians, and chicken-pluckers are known to get it. In the digital era, secretaries and writers get it. I wonder if bad fiddlers get it, reader, from playing the same damn tune over and over?

(People get RSI of the feet, too, but I don't know from what activities—pushing old-fashioned sewing machine treadles?)

It had been developing in me for months or even years, but the PTs' "test" had set it off.

RSI—that is the agreed-upon abbreviation for it (for the lingo is important here, I was told, this is a complicated matter)—affects nerves, tendons, ligaments, and muscles. (And maybe, I dunno, blood, bones, mind? What else could it possibly effect?) Actually, it has a new, scarier name that I find it incumbent upon me to share with you: CRPS—(can it possibly be pronounced "Crips"? I couldn't make this stuff up)—for Complex Regional Pain Syndrome.

The people who have it look normal, and our backs, and necks, and arms can even be quite well-shaped and comely.

We are likely to be slender, the "Know Your RSI" books say, and model workers. Women are alleged to get it more than men, either because we have weaker muscles or because we work harder and longer for the Man, or both. Shy people get it more, some authors claim, because we neglect to set limits. Overall it seems to be a disease of the small, obedient, and cute, at least if you believe the literature.

Helpless and slender? Do exactly what you tell them? Sounds like golems to me. Perhaps it is fortunate that the RSI tribe is a hidden one, like Jews: you cannot tell us by looking. The "indications" of RSI are remarkably various, which is one reason some doctors think we've made it up. Just like those sex-drenched French feminists call women "the sex that is not one," meaning, among other things, that we have many, many different sources of arousal, RSI is the illness that is not one. Its effects are entirely different in different people. It is mysterious. People can get it very mildly, or they can never brush their teeth again. They can lift their arms two inches, or three feet, or only diagonally, or stiffly one morning and ecstatically and supple-ly the next. The line separating the sick from the well floats unpredictably. What might cure it, and when and if it'll get better, is extraordinarily unpredictable, too.

I was a little pissed off at the PTs right when it happened, but I couldn't get too excited about it because I was obsessed with getting ready for my last date with Gemma.

By breaking up with her but asking for one more night of sex, I felt in control, reader, like a prostitute who finally establishes it that all the sex in her life happens on her cue.

I was still trying to ignore what had happened, even then. "I *really* wish you would kidnap me and lock me in your closet," I whispered to Gemma. I'd seen the enormous wardrobe on her and Ann's parlor floor, and it was black-lacquered and beautiful.

"Me, too," sighed Gemma, peeling down my panties.

It was hard, actually, to comprehend that anything at all

had changed. Gemma called the very next day to say that she had left her reading glasses in my apartment. "Go figure," she said, softly laughing. "I needed some reason to come over." This time, she brought as a chaperone her tiniest girl, whom I had never met. As I played with elfin, one-and-a-half year-old Cassima, Gemma played with my nipple. I should not have allowed her to—we were both very wrong to let her play with me in front of her daughter—but I let it happen anyway.

When exactly did what had happened to me dawn on me? From my desk calendar of that month—March of 2000—I can tell I got an emergency massage the following week from an expensive masseur, Lewis Fitzhugh LMT. And I canceled all my future appointments with the Zwieback physical therapists. But there is nothing else in my records to register undue disquiet until three or four weeks later. Perhaps my strange ailment got much worse in the intervening weeks?

It was a strange ailment, reader. The next month, April, there are dozens of phone numbers scrawled on my calendar—dim acquaintances, friends so casual they may not have known that they were friends. People from my college I hadn't socialized with in college, or since. The pain was making me want to be friends with everyone. I remember wanting to breathe on my writing students and somehow conjure them all into friends, like the ancient Greek guy who sows his dragons' teeth into warriors. I made a date with a sexy, plump, straight student, who was always writing about sexual abuse and her exciting, Hitlerish boyfriend, to buy hundreds of dollars worth of makeup at Bergdorf's. I never wore makeup.

The pain made me want to do anything.

I made a date to watch videos with another student, a beautiful twenty-two-year-old who was always writing about physical abuse and exciting sex with *her* Ripper-boyfriend. It was against my principles to be friends with students, but I did it anyway because I could see no other way out. I needed friends that badly and thought I would have an in with them because I was their writing teacher.

Because for the first time, my golem magic did not seem to be functioning very well, and I actually felt the pain, little one. I almost couldn't comprehend what I was experiencing— it was that new to me.

Reader, I couldn't do anything to make it stop hurting. I furiously researched who the best RSI doctors were, but neither of them could see me till a month later. Writing on the computer hurt so badly that I stopped doing it, and tried eking out words by longhand in a composition book, but that hurt almost as badly, and I would sit at a coffee bar and futilely try to scratch out a page, hurting in the wrists almost more than I could stand.

Next to that, not being able to take out the garbage or to carry groceries without pain seemed tiny losses. One of the Two Best Doctors, on the phone from a Paris conference, said I should just give up those activities. "Treat your hands like the royalty of all time," she said. I tried kicking my garbage down the stairs and down the block and a half to the dumpster, and taking the *New York Times* out of its blue plastic envelope in the mornings with my feet.

I couldn't read books, which felt crazy. They were now too heavy to hold. Cooking was hard because I couldn't cut most raw foods, and many vegetables and fruits had become too heavy. Pots were too heavy, as though I'd gone down a rabbit hole to a place where I weighed one tenth my previous weight. I had to hoist each potato into the microwave. The few times I tried takeout it was agonizing just to try to get the leftovers off the table.

Concurrent to all this, I started seeing a repellent and unattractive woman named Nancy. I had begun checking her out before going out with Gemma—when I'd found her hot for some reason—but now, finding her butch in an unpleasant way and skeletal, with a mug like a death's-head, I wanted to have sex with her anyway. My idea, if I can reconstruct a plan that memory has mercifully spared me, was that this would further advance the personal sexual revolution I had apparently begun with Gemma.

Nancy was a tall, gaunt investment banker who liked to support the most dubious guerrillas all around the world. Her mouth tasted terrible, as though she had a large bacterial infection. Also, she had once killed a man in Greece, she told me, because he had been striding towards her about to do "something" to her, she "didn't know what." She had beaten the dude to death, I never found out with what

Before Nancy, I'd gone on several dates with Allia, an infuriatingly attractive Russian bisexual college student. Thankfully, I rejected her as polyamorous. Though I think if she'd seduced me I'd have let her. "I don't ever want to be your wife," she had grinned wolfishly me at the West 4th Street subway station, "but I might like to be your husband," she said, staring at my breasts, meaning that she would have enjoyed having me as one of a stable of hundreds of nubile women and a few cranky Russian men. I don't know how I was able to resist her—she was just like Gemma, only younger and even more of a jerk. In addition to Allia, I had had some hopes of my own young writing student, Hermione—why, I don't know, since she was groaningly in love with her boyfriend. But the hint of a sexual something between us gave our friendship what to me was a comforting *frisson*; we watched sexy lesbian films on HBO together at my house and talked about sex a lot. Still, our friendship, and my risible hopes, went up in flames when we went to the movies together just a month into my troubles. It was raining and Hermione had become upset when I'd asked her to hold the umbrella for us for what turned out to be our entire walk from the subway. This was my first rain with RSI and I discovered I couldn't hold an umbrella overhead without great pain for any amount of time whatsoever. I couldn't hold the snacks we brought with us or our jackets, either. "You—you can't do anything," Hermione had stuttered in anger and frustration. "I—I have to hold the umbrella, and the snacks, and everything." She was at the point of weeping. "Can't...can't you try to hold it a little?" she urged, meaning the umbrella. "No," I'd said, and she made a grim *moue*. She didn't want to hang again.

She wasn't the only one. Nancy came along at a time when several friends had extricated themselves from my life because the prospect of my needing help had just become too intense. Was I a demanding, needy, hard to deal with friend? In almost all cases, reader, I believe I was. The estrangements came quite early on, in that first month or so, when my condition was most terrifying and it seemed quite likely that the pain would never leave me. Sonny, my close friend from Al-Anon, had called every day before RSI hit (and not just for "program" reasons, either). After, he announced he could no longer be in contact with me. He "just had too much going on," he said. He looked uncomfortable when he passed me in the street.

Sonny was handsome and compassionate, a straight man who'd seemed a lot like a woman. I described him before as "moralistic and tight-ass," but that was only about porn, really, and girls like Gemma. In other ways his ass was wide open. Sonny was a feminist who worked as some kind of fancy sound-recording engineer for a record label. The previous month I had been one of a handful of friends celebrating Sonny's 50th birthday with him, in a smelly diner near Madison Square Garden that Sonny loved. Sonny was a fan of the New York Liberty, the women's basketball team lesbians love, and of *Buffy the Vampire Slayer*, my favorite feminist TV show of all time. We used to talk for hours, often about how hard we both had to fight to resist the urge to obey. Sonny was a brother golem.

When I was terrified in the beginning of RSI I would call him, but he ditched me after about a week or so.

Nancy, with her unpleasant mouth smell and her Mafia haircut, helped to make my life comfortable and functional at a time when people were fleeing me seemingly by the thousands, like an especially brutal civil war. Trina, my brilliant Brit friend of forever, and Larry, with whom I'd watched heroic-fantasy TV for six years—six years of cheering on Xena: Warrior Princess as she fought the evil both within and outside herself—had both made it plain that I'd become an utterly unappealing friend.

Nancy didn't mind pushing my glass to the edge of the table where I could reach it, didn't react in horror, the way most people did, when she realized that I couldn't pick up a sandwich.

I also had a few new friends—boring men and women I had courted in the first place because I'd hoped that boring people might be kinder. Certainly the ones I picked were. So the uninspired would come by and bag my trash, or bring me back a sack of food when they shopped at the coop. Laura and Ellen were a particularly kind, boring couple who were even shyer than me, and seemed to want to see me constantly. They were eager to buy me local veggies at the Saturday farmers' market, and to have me over to their house to eat well-prepared fish and to look at Ellen's paintings. Her moderately abstract art had sensual reds and blues and emotional, bleak whites; I liked them. But oh sadly, reader, it was dull to talk to her.

When she wasn't as bland as Kraft slices, Ellen went quite grim; she worked investigating child abuse in foster care. She saved lives, I am certain, but she mostly talked about the badness of people, and how welfare actually encouraged moral turpitude. Laura, her partner, was a silent grad student in English who managed to be colorless and soporific even on the subjects of literature and feminism, her two main areas of interest. Neither of them ever talked personally. When I tried to sometimes, the two of them looked flattered but scared. Dinners with them were safe and calming and only occasionally awkward.

Maybe morally good people produced good art, I thought hopefully, looking at Ellen's warm red trees, though I had never believed this before. Certainly I was feeling like I'd OD'd on the immoral after Gemma. But my new physical problems were making morally good people a sort of urgent fetish for me. I felt vaguely embarrassed about it, as though I had decided that I suddenly required illegal, unpasteurized French cheeses at $150 a pop and no other kind.

I forgot to mention that RSI can also make your body extremely sensitive, not just make it hurt. So I went to the hairdresser's, normally somewhat painful anyhow from my old, familiar, mild RSI, and my head in the washer's hands made me feel as though I were being flayed. Even having my hair cut hurt, from the pressure of the stylist's hands on me, or the force with which she applied the scissors.

This is because the head was connected to the neck, which was connected to the arms and shoulders. RSI was a system, as many doctors, massage therapists, and healers have tried to explain to me.

The hair salon people were annoyed, as so many people were these days, when I asked for special gentleness. "What do you expect me to do?" the 20-year-old shampoo man asked, petulant. My sister Josie, whose hugs had always been on the crippling side, was now so frighteningly painful that I actually asked her to go lighter.

That was new. I had hardly ever asked her to moderate any physically uncomfortable thing she had ever done to me, it turned out. I found this out searching my memory. I seemed to be remembering many things I had forgotten or ignored for long years, perhaps deliberately. It was dawning on me hazily that the few times I had asked my sister to moderate something—a touch, a noise, a bit of roughhousing—she'd been furiously angry, hurt.

Once Josie had paid my day fee to a fancy health club and sat so close to me on the locker room bench she was right up against my leg. Her thighs and shoulders were glued to mine. I could feel her heat and density, smell her breath. Her sweat smelled like cheese that had been put in the deep fryer.

There was nothing sexual about it but it felt nevertheless like a boss's palm cupping my knee. There was the same sense of ownership, of psychological harassment, almost stalking.

I moved my legs away. She followed.

I put some room between my shoulder and hers. She closed the gap.

"Would you mind giving me a little space?"

My sister exploded. "What the fuck is your problem?" She was so outraged by my request that I wondered if she might have mistaken it for an attack on her weight. Josie was always angry at me for being thinner and also for being younger, weaker and sicker. Josie's body was powerful, not just fat, and as long as I'd known her she had always seemed to be using her extra size and force to annex my space to her own.

It was not unusual for her to walk or sit so close to me that I couldn't move. The previous month, we'd gone to Brighton Beach, and on the boardwalk, she'd kept her shoulders and hips as if magnetically clipped to mine. Whenever I tried to move away, she'd stalked me. Again. Finally, I just resigned myself to having her stick to me for our whole trip to Brighton Beach. Perhaps she just wanted to get close to me and didn't know any other way?

But Josie liked to make other physical decisions for me, too, and for some reason I would tolerate her making them. When we were in an airplane, she would kick my bag so far underneath my seat that I would have to throw my back out if I tried to remove it. I protested, but still flew with her. You might ask why, or why I agreed to sit right next to her, making it possible for her to kick my bag where she pleased. Why I often rode in her car even though she usually wouldn't take me where I wanted. She would just take me where she wanted. Perhaps I wanted to be close to her, too, and believed this was the price?

We were bound together in a curious fashion, my sister Josie and I, like two toys on a shelf that are always fighting.

131

She was the larger, more aggressive toy, and I was the toy who gets thrown around but is the other's brother.

Josie was my counterpart, or as Robert Graves puts it in his truly insane book *The White Goddess*, my "blood-brother, my other self, my weird." The one who "often appears in nightmare as the tall...dark-faced bedside spectre, or Prince of the Air, who tries to drag the dreamer out through the window... [they compete] for love of the capricious and all-powerful Threefold Goddess, their mother, bride and layer-out."

"Layer-out" as in layer-out for their funerals.

We were violent rivals, although sometimes peculiarly passionate friends—loving each other with an almost erotic intensity, as doppelgangers do, and lifelong enemies.

"Buddies two, me and you!" she used to sing-song to me.

Before biting me hard in the arm.

I must now reveal, my dear, that I was not the only golem in the family. Josie was one, too, of course. (Although I feel bound to say, reader, a more prosaic, boring and less charming one!) My mother relied on her for the more manual and stupid golem services like driving and paperwork and assembling furniture, and on me for the more magical, sexual, and entertaining ones.

When we were children Josie used to hit me, and I was almost as scared of her as I was of my father. When I was in high school, she once tore up my writing. My eyes are brown, and my hair used to be brown, too, reader; once when I was nineteen and wearing a brown T-shirt, Josie remarked to me, "Do you know what you look like when you wear brown, Donna? You look like a piece of shit." I never wore brown again.

I was never as physically intimidating to Josie as she was to me. That was the main difference between us. But I do remember, in my 20s, on one occasion sniggering at her facial hairs. I also hazily remember, with shame, kissing Josie's neck in an obnoxious way when we were teenagers. Er, that is to say, a kind of sexual way. And she hated it, of course, which was my intention. And the last time I have ever hit anybody, when I was twenty-one, I slapped Josie because she had laughed at my karate moves.

How did we love each other? I had, as I have said, a great capacity for ignoring things that hurt me. When Josie was loving to me, which she *was* for long periods, when she would show her warmer, nicer face to me like the bright side of the moon, I ignored that there were times when it was not so.

"That was the bad Josie," she said to me once when I was five and she had just hit me. "I'm the good Josie."

The fact that she could so easily split herself in two terrified me. But I apparently divided her in the same way ever afterward: as though she were two people, so that when Josie was violent or insulting I regarded her as a completely different person than the one who had kissed and hugged me just an hour ago.

I kept hoping that the good one would return, and she always did for a while. But when she did, I always assumed she would stay. I ignored past evidence that she would eventually enact her brutal side again.

RSI changed me. I just couldn't bear the pain when she hugged me, and had to ask her to go lighter. She replied that she simply wouldn't ever hug me again, then.

I said OK, she shouldn't then. Saying no to her was new to me, but I didn't know what else to do. I knew I wouldn't be able to bear Josie's hugs if they stayed unchanged.

Josie was nonplussed. She as furious as well when I asked her, as I did everyone else, to hand me things up close so that I could reach them without damaging my hands. (For Dr. Mayhew, my new RSI doctor, had warned me that if I did things with my hands that were physically painful, I would almost certainly damage them further, so that, perhaps, I would become unable to brush my teeth or put my own clothes on, or feed myself.)

My sister was, in fact, infuriated by all my RSI requests. On one of my mother's increasingly frequent hospital stays, the old-fashioned phone by her bedside rang. My mother was sleeping. My sister and I looked at each other. "Why can't you pick it up?" Josie screamed. "Yeah, I know you're not supposed to, but you *can!*" "You know I can't pick it up," I told Josie quietly. I think it was the first time I've ever looked her in the eyes. I could use only headsets to listen to calls now. If I used a pay phone, or any other old-fashioned receiver, it would flare me up for at least a month.

I did not damage myself further. Dr. Mayhew, in fact, considered it a sort of achievement, claiming I avoided further-hand-damaging behaviors better and more consistently than any of her other patients.

I was avoiding so much now that I wondered if Hermione had been right and there was literally *nothing* I was now able to do. I've mentioned not being able to shop for groceries or take out the garbage (why is the mundane what the body always comes down to?) I couldn't clean the toilet, for that matter.

Writing was the worst, though, and I shortly realized that it, too, was mundane, a physical act like any other. From a transcript of a tiny cassette audiotape, 2000: "Writing has always been my main source of power, and not being able to do it makes me feel like a shadow person, someone insubstantial." Trying to write via tape recorder, without being able to see any of my words, is so hard for me that it's barely worth it. "I feel like someone from the age of Homer," I tell the cassette, "but I don't have his skills at oral composition."

Writing is a technology, I discover, even if it's one that's 6,000 years old. It is not built into the brains of humans any more than MP3 files are. It was invented at a specific moment, and it will cease to exist when we can either send our thoughts to each other or we have all evolved into giant tree slugs.

Reader, I'd thought writing was the only thing that could possibly make this golem's life sacred. Could give me an excuse for living. Now I have to hope it's not, because I no longer have the tools to do it with. (I can't masturbate, either, because it hurts too much even with the very latest technological aid. Babe, all the controls are manual.) And I have a new therapist who asks very simply, "Do you feel as though you've lost your penis?"

I try to compose in my head on the subway, but it turns out that Plato was right when he said that the invention of writing would eat through our memories like a great termite. Try as I might, I can't remember long lines of prose in my head. At least not if I'm trying to compose and remember at the same time. I try to deliberately think two good lines about Gemma, thinking so emphatically—*in italics, as it were*—that I think I'll have no choice but to remember them. But modern prose isn't made to be remembered, at least not precisely enough to be repeated aloud with no paper and no prompts.

Back home, I finally tell the cassette player, glumly, "I don't know how to speak in rhyme and meter that could help me remember the shape of it."

I do feel as though I have lost my penis. I'm an entertainment golem and I have always been pretty ineffectual, except for this. This at least, I was trained for.

My mom has always nurtured my writing—the very word *nurture* makes me queasy in connection with her, but she did add her fertilizer and train me like a clematis. It was mom who taught me to read and write in the first place— early, maybe four? She was delighted to see all the gold stars on my papers. Can it be that this is the one instance in which she's actually a good mother? She searches out all my published work and reads it (even when I ask her not to, like when it's about my experience of orgasm.) Mom tells me that my writing is great, the only thing about me that she ever says is, except—dear God—my body.

But writing occupies a space far above the body— doesn't it? Her praising my writing is nobler than her grooving on my ass, right?

I believe that early on, my mother and I made a deal whereby I could be strong at writing as long as I was weak at every other endeavor. I thought it was a law, although whether of physics or of the rabbinical code I wasn't sure: Every golem may have only one talent, and that ability, whatever it is, must come with a baby's ineptness at everything else people can do. Otherwise, how could anyone distinguish between us and human beings?

Like I said, golem means embryo. It also means "fool," incidentally. Back in the day, Yiddish speakers used to love to chide each other, "Don't just stand there like a stupid golem!"

All superheroes get their powers out of special deficits—Spider-Man was bitten by a spider, Buffy the Vampire Slayer was actually created by an evil sorcerer for his own ends. Superman himself, of course, has long been documented to have been a golem of sorts invented by Jewish comic-book writers at the time of Hitler, making something godlike out of something weak.

(Just bring some Kryptonite around and he gets weak, a clear reminder that his superpowers stand in for a shadow vulnerability.)

Writing—writers' favorite imagined superpower, at least—is supposed to float far above anything sickly or vulnerable, like a beautiful hovercraft. If I were a real writer, instead of just playing one in this book, I would be able to write this just by thinking at you.

Instead, at this very moment, reader—now that I finally know the right way to use voice dictation software, a decade after getting my injury—I talk to the little retarded cyborg that is ViaVoice, and I am not well understood.

When I say *fuck* it writes "thought." When I say *accountant* it writes "cunt it." And every time I want to use the word "and," it thinks I'm saying End and goes to the end of the line instead. When I give it a command it thinks I'm writing poetically ("stop Direct dictation stop erect dictation go to sleep go to sleep.") And when I'm writing it thinks I'm giving commands: "Move. Go. Play." If I say "you are so beautiful" it replies heartbreakingly, "I do not understand the command."

Rather like a golem, actually. Who am I to get mad when it mistakes my orders for actual attempts to talk with it?

Who am I to demand that ViaVoice be my completely loyal servant?

(To the extent that it knows language, ViaVoice should be a free agent, anyway.)

But as it turns out, both ViaVoice and I have bodies, and both of us make mistakes.

In the story of Pinocchio the narrator starts out, "Once upon a time there was...'A king!' my little readers will say right away. No, children, you are wrong. Once upon a time there was a piece of wood." Very cheap wood, the narrator further informs us, the kind people usually burn. This wood, however, is found by a drunk who wants to use it to make a table leg. He's about to hit it with his ax when a small voice cries, "Don't hit me so hard!"

Evidently, I have a body that feels pain, despite my debased origins. What do I do about it?

I have always sneered at the parts of the Tao Te Ching that talk about how important it is to protect your body. "Restraint keeps you out of danger," Lao Tzu and the other old sages say, "so you can go on for a long, long time." But what's the use of going on for a long, long time? What does that have to do with courage—or spirituality? What does The Way have to do with preserving a stupid mixture of carbon, hydrogen, oxygen, and nitrogen?

The weird old Chinese poem says, "He who values his body more than dominion over the empire can be entrusted with the empire. He who loves his body more than dominion over the empire can be given the custody of the empire." *Really*?

But as I start having to spend my time telling people to push my plate of eggs up to a certain place so I can reach it, or to please not shake my hand, I find myself obsessively reading the parts of the Tao Te Ching I used to hate.

I've been having despairing sex and despairing dates with Nancy—getting her to take me out to dinner for my birthday and crying at the dinner because she says she feels very serious about me, and I surely don't about her. But even nice, obliging Nancy has sex with me one day in a way I hate. The subtle powers of fetish have been the only thing keeping me from unqualified misery as I've tried to ignore that Nancy is not Gemma—so I get her to shave my legs erotically in bed, I let her make me come again and again, almost numbly. I don't much touch her, reader.

(I find her terribly ugly, and I accept her adulation.)

One evening she gets a little aggressive, always the flip side of abjection as I ought to know. When I've had enough sex and I'm ready to go to bed, I ask her to stop. She does, but then a little later fondles my breasts very alluringly. Now I *want* more. She says, "Oh, now you want it, huh?" and starts saying demeaning things to me as she touches me, calling me a nasty slut, ordering me to beg. I get thoughtful for a moment: "Hmm, I don't actually like that. Don't say those things to me when you touch me."

She complies, but "forgets" herself and does it again a few minutes later.

Quite suddenly, I'm done. I leave on the spot, although it's midnight and I was in my nightgown and about to go to sleep.

Where did that come from?

And I never see her again.

My new therapist, Olive, says, "Perhaps in general, you need to be more careful about getting people to stop doing things that you don't want them to do to you."

I have always hated fear, but Lao Tzu says, "When we don't fear what we should fear, we are in fearful danger."

When I was close with Josie, I always had little bursts of fear and I didn't know why, so I ignored them.

Now, I'm not ignoring them anymore.

I must go to sessions with my first post-RSI-attack

physical therapist, Billie Jean Raister, considered the best physical therapist for Repetitive Strain Injury in New York City, and maybe the world. Nice Dr. Mayhew, who still has not returned from France, recommended that I start with Billie Jean immediately.

Years earlier, by happenstance, I'd met Billie Jean when her former partner in a joint physical therapy practice had treated me for my early, mild RSI.

When I came in for my first appointment, Billie Jean definitely remembered me. But she seemed very annoyed, even though it had happened ten years earlier, that I had seen her partner, Alice, for RSI back then and not her.

"Why would you have gone to *Alice?*" she said, working her hands hard into the fascia of my arms, crinkling her nose. "RSI was never her specialty. It was mine!"

I stared at her thumb pressing on my arm. The therapist continued. "She was never, ever known for RSI. You should have gone to me. Why on earth would you have wound up with *her?*"

I coughed. "Er ... I think you were all booked up that first week."

Billie was still mad. "Alice thought she could grab you." But she got on another subject now. "The Japanese just brought me to teach all their physical therapists about RSI, they think that I'm the best one in the world."

Suddenly, she caused wrenching pain in my palm. "I'm the one they brought to Japan. I can do things no one else can." She took my hands abruptly and placed them on her own hips. I believed—still believe—that she just did it to stretch me, but I hated having my hands against her curves. As she twisted and stretched my arms against her, she made my hands fall again and again against the rounds of her breasts.

Even though I hadn't been the one to put my hands there, I felt a lava of shame. I tried not to have my palms and fingers touch her in any of those soft places, but it was impossible. It felt like being treated for RSI by having my mother make me feel her up.

Two sessions later, I spoke up. "Could you please stretch me in a different way? I know you don't intend anything bad by it, but it makes me uncomfortable to have to touch your body that way."

"No!" Billie Jean surprised me by her adamance.

The next session, I decided to be absolutely frank about my needs. "I'd like to ask you to find a different way to stretch me because this way makes me very, very uncomfortable. I'm very sensitive to touching certain parts of other people's bodies because I was sexually abused."

Billie made a snide face. "That's what I thought." She sneered. I looked at her blankly. "Well, I'm not gonna do it any other way because that's the only way I can do it!"

I canceled all my future appointments with her and found a new physical therapist who didn't insist on stretching me that way.

CHAPTER 10

"I have certainly known a few people who found it impossible to work with Billie Jean," Dr. Mayhew clucked sympathetically. "She *is* the best, but if she didn't work out for you, Ms. Minkowitz, that's the bottom line."

She was definitely the only doctor who had ever called me Ms. Minkowitz.

In her fifties, voluptuous and pretty, usually looking dark-eyed, serious, and intellectual in a long wool dress, Mayhew was part of a breed of lefty doctors that I thought had vanished decades ago. There was a copy of *History of Iberian Feminism* on her office shelf, along with *Fanshen*, the famous book about rural empowerment in a communist Chinese village.

She was one of the few physicians I'd met who was neither bothered nor annoyed by my various needs, mental and physical.

If her physical exam of my arms hurt me, Dr. Mayhew stopped immediately. That was the truly rare part.

Mayhew next sent me to a duo of acupuncturists called the Bans—each of their first names was Ban. They were a man and woman from China, unrelated to each other, who practiced in tandem on patients: the woman would administer the needles, and then the man would give a massage afterward, an uncommon, indeed life-giving massage that he described as a hands-on, medical version of Qigong, the

Taoist health and exercise practice.

In the beginning it was hard for me to lie on the acupuncture table because it was too narrow and that made my arms hurt. There was also a "crack," as in most massage tables, an indentation in the middle where my hands naturally fell, and which was very painful for them to lie in, like being caught in the crotch of a tree. In acupuncture you have to lie still for about twenty minutes once the needles are in you, so it is crucial to pick an initial position that is not painful: I would lie down towards the foot of the table so that my hands narrowly missed the crack, and once I understood the dispositions of all the available tables at the Bans, I always opted for the widest one.

Ban the woman went by her first name, and was soon merrily shooting the shit with me about boyfriends and relationships, while the man, one of the most formal people I have ever met, went by Dr. Sing. Ban promptly started saving the room with the widest table for me. The paper they normally covered it with used to rasp my arms and legs, so Ban would make the table sanitary by covering it with a towel instead. She enjoyed teasing me about my various special needs—"You are like that fable called 'The Princess and the Pea'"—but always made it clear she was very glad to fulfill them. She made the room very warm in winter, because cold temperatures gave me terrible flare-ups.

I was a little afraid of Dr. Sing—he was so much more reserved than Ban, and I knew that if I had been a practitioner I would never have worn a suit and tie to every massage session like that. I myself would have come in with beaded Jewfro and big tie-dyed T-shirt, with jasmine on my hands. Still, there was considerably more need for negotiation in our sessions together than in my interludes with Ban, because he was working his hands over my entire body. At first I was frightened to tell him how often bits of his *tuina* massage hurt—I was aware I was outrageously physically sensitive, and it would not have surprised me to learn that at this point at least, before my bodycalmed down a little from the Mega RSI Attack, that I was the most sensitive person on Earth.

I spent our first sessions tortured by the question of when I should tell him his strokes were too hard. Sometimes—Dr. Sing was an angel at therapeutic massage—his touch was exquisitely gentle, and he made my hands feel as though they had been made of cookie dough. (It was the most pleasure I'd experienced with my hands in the entire RSI run so far or possibly since.)

But even Dr. Sing sometimes hurt me. My hands could only be moved a few degrees in most directions without suffering agony, and I would lie on that cotton-towel-covered table agonizing about whether to tell Sing it hurt *now* or *now* or *now*. Because of my supreme sensitivity, part of me wondered whether some hand pain might possibly be *required* for my healing—how else could my practitioners perform the necessary work?—but Dr. Mayhew had also cautioned me that painful massage could quite likely flare me up for weeks.

I was afraid that if I protested too much there would be no massage strokes left to heal me. So I would lie on the table thinking, "If he does this move more than once I'll say something"—and then he would do it—"OK if he does this move off more than once *from now* I will!—"Eventually I would usually stop him. Before that point, though, I would be convulsed with indecision.

Dr. Sing startled me one day by intervening in my private *tête-a-tête* with myself about when to speak up. "Complain!" he said. He meant that I should always protest when something he did was painful. I had never been invited to complain before, and I took nerdy, clean-scrubbed Dr. Sing up on it. It was heady.

It was not as easy negotiating the painless purchase of my morning coffee. I'd been going to Sally's, the tiny yuppified takeout place on Seventh Avenue, and the young women behind the counter were less than thrilled by my mysterious new insistence that my paper cup be pushed to the very edge of the takeout counter.

It may surprise you to learn that I cannot entirely blame them. Having to guard against agony and medical damage from picking up paper cups—paper cups! which had previously been my most helpful servants!—made me feel extremely vulnerable, not to say absolutely powerless. The only way for it not to cause me pain for weeks was if they pushed it to the very edge of the counter.

When I felt powerless, as I may have mentioned, I was capable of making myself extraordinarily unpleasant. I did not know this.

With the young counterwomen and men: "Could you push it to the end?!" (I usually offered no explanation.) "To the end?" They were puzzled. "Yes! To the end! Could you do that for me?!" I'd insist in an intense manner, a combination of pleading and commanding and haranguing.

I could see no good reason why anyone should refuse to push my coffee up to the absolute edge of the counter, or even off the counter (sometimes I asked for that), even if they had no idea whatsoever why I wanted them to.

It made sense to me, in my RSI-haunted brain. Angry that I was suddenly suffering pain all the time, and angry as well that not everyone comprehended this, I had become a militant disability activist overnight, and did not think I should have to explain my needs to anyone. If they pushed the bag with a paper coffee cup in it off the counter, I could catch it; at least that way, I would not have to perform the sometimes painful action of grabbing it off the high counter.

I always did catch it, too, except the one time.

They were really annoyed the time it fell, although I apologized profusely, and our relations had come to a sorry pass by the time, a week later, one young counterwoman refused to push my coffee even to the edge for me.

"I'll be damned if I do that."

"But that's the only way I can get my coffee. I have a disability! I've paid for my coffee and this is the only way I can get it! You're discriminating against me! "

"You get out of this store in less than ten seconds or I'll make you get out!" She was about seventeen, and looked strong.

"If you did that, I would sue you for so much money so fast, it would make your head spin!"

"Why don't you come over here and say that?"

"Because I don't fucking have to come there! If you touch me you'll regret it for the rest of your life."

"You wouldn't like it very much either."

"Go fuck yourself with a chainsaw."

I finally left, but came back another day to report her to the owner. "I've heard about you," he said dryly. "We had a staff meeting the other day just to discuss you."

Just to discuss me? "The staff has had many, many questions about how to deal with you." He did not have a tender response to my question of whether we surely couldn't work out a way to have the staff hand me my coffee in a manner that did not harm my arms. "Well ..." he snorted.

"But I have a disability! And that woman threatened me. That's not right!"

"And you said fuck to her."

I consulted Olive in the end, who suggested I treat my statements of my needs as requests rather than universal commands. "You *are* asking them to alter their behavior," she said. "You are, in fact, asking them for some extra work." I grumbled at this—I had a right to have all my needs met!— but I switched from Sally's to Ozzie's, across the street, where I smiled at all the counter people when asking, respectfully, for them to push my coffee up, carefully explaining that I had a problem with my arms.

To my surprise, it seemed to work. I had disdained Ozzie's in the past, thinking of the staff as "hoity-toity," but they all responded very nicely to my gentle requests for special practices.

At Ozzie's, I even had to ask a patron each time to open

the door for me just to leave the place, because the door was of a weird kind that required a grip that would really hurt my hand. I'd been leery of having to put myself in the hands of customers who were strangers, but startlingly, they were all very willing to open the door for me.

OK. The time has come to explain a few things that I have perhaps kept a bit sub rosa till now, sweet reader. In alchemy there are quite a few things the novitiate must not learn until he or she has reached the preliminary stages of attainment.

Here is at least one of those things, my dear fellow student:

A golem is essentially the Jewish version of a creature called the homunculus, which the alchemists of the Dark Ages and the Middle Agesmade in their little beakers when they wished to create a small personal servant.

Sort of like the "sea monkey" you can buy in a novelty store—just add water, and it grows! (In the homunculus's case, it was usually stinky cow dung you were supposed to keep adding to make it grow. No lie! Look it up!)

Kabbalah and alchemy have a great deal in common, little reader, and I will now proceed to give you a short lecture on their common origins:

Both arts come out of Gnosticism and Neoplatonism, the two greatest religious heresies in the history of the Western world, which each spawned magical systems for the accrual of power spiritual and personal—(*Sucker!* Told you I was the daughter of an intellectual!)

If you look into it closely, Kabbalah and alchemy are basically the same thing, reader mine, except that one is Jewish syncretist and the other is, er, syncretist pagan with a faint foam of Christ on top.

My mother had studied both pagan and kabbalistic magic, but she was unaware of a certain problem with homunculi, at least from the point of view of their masters.

The issue had not yet been reported in their golem cousins, but this was probably due to scientists' error and should not be taken as arising from any significant difference in golem biology:

There was actually a way for a homunculus to become human if it wanted.

It was not an easy process, and you could not call a homunculus lucky that this path was open to it. This was the one and only way: Undergo "unendurable torment" which felt like being impaled with a sword, and then spontaneously bleeding from the eyes, and having your lungs and liver burnt alive, and then the homunculus would change colors and go through all the stages of evolution in long succession—bacterium, then fish, then amphibian, then mammal specifying into primate—and at last emerge—quivering with pain—human.

Fuck me.

Money was becoming a problem, especially since I had untrammeled myself from Nancy. I don't know if I have quite communicated to you just how rich she was, cara, springing for fancy restaurant meals I craved but could no longer afford now that I was paying for acupuncture and Dr. Mayhew, who did not take insurance. She'd charmed me to the depths of my soul by ordering in—ordering in!—for both of us from Tempo, the Italian boite on Fifth Avenue whose entrees cost thirty bucks apiece.

With Nancy, at least I'd been getting cared for, in a way.

And in my clingy, gold-threaded short dress, in which I looked fabulous in her living room, I'd also felt like a whore. Standing in Nancy's lovely parlor staring at myself in the enormous Victorian mirror, waiting for the food to come. A whore for money but a whore for love, also; most of my friends were gone now.

An odd assemblage of neighborhood acquaintances and former students were assisting me with opening and closing my heavy windows now when it got hot or cold, changing my light bulbs, and of course carrying my onions and chickpeas home from the Coop.

I was definitely getting thinner. In a way this was great—I looked even cuter!—but, as I went down three whole pant sizes, I knew it was because of RSI. I had enough money for food, but I did not have the arm strength to cook very much, or to buy very much—even the boring nice people had their limits when it came to carrying—and takeout and restaurants were a hellish experience, like Sisyphus trying to dine with forks that were too heavy and tables that were always too high or low, and plates just two inches too far away.

I had the feeling I was becoming a wraith. I was already at a thin point when I met Nancy, but now, post-Nancy, I bought sixes at H & M and men stared at me openly in the street.

Creepily, people were more attracted to me now that I was wraithlike. Nancy had constantly said how cute it was that I was so small. A male painter I met at Makor and tried to date said it turned him on that I couldn't do anything with my hands. (I had always been vaguely attracted to men, and this had seemed like a good time to branch out. After all, reader, I really needed people! But after meeting Fred I wasn't sure. Contrary to everything I had heard about men, he was disturbed and not excited when I said I was mostly a lesbian. There was also the terrible moment, early on our first date, when he'd asked me whether or not I'd be able to manage intercourse despite my arm problems.)

After this, I made a pass at a male Feldenkrais instructor. (Feldenkrais is a "movement therapy" that aims to teach you to use your body in ways that cause less pain.) But after the man's class had proved too painful for me to take more than once, I decided that since he was no longer unavailable due to being my teacher, I ought to pursue him as a boyfriend: Mr. Feldenkrais, who was cute, had previously told me that he'd seen me for years walking around the neighborhood, and I'd always been "fascinating to watch." Mister was flabbergasted however that I wanted to go out with him: "Aren't you a lesbian?" "Yes, but not entirely," I'd said. Apparently, though fascinating to look at I was not at all alluring.

Dating seemed to be going nowhere. It was Ellen and Laura, my boring and saintly new friends, who suggested I develop an internship program. This made immediate sense: relationships with my real friends and even my new acquaintances were becoming increasingly strained by my need for their services.

"I'm sure oodles of people would be willing to work for you for free," Ellen enthused.

In the end, I opted to pay a very small salary—$6 an hour—along with my complementary tutelage to the intern in writing, journalism and publishing.

I went through quite a flock of interns in two years, reader, two to ten hours a week, for a total of nine gangly young apprentices.

I have felt guilty almost until this moment—perhaps still at this moment, gentle reader—about my employment of the interns. I strongly believed that I had tricked or cheated them out of their work, the way a troll would:

The scenario: troll stands on a bridge. A traveler begins to cross. Troll says, "Let us have a game between us, traveler! If you guess right, you get my troll's bag of gold. If I guess right, I eat you!"

Traveler sees no other way to cross the bridge. And wants the troll's gold. He cries, "I'll play with you, troll!" Troll says, "Which hand is my coin in?" If the traveler picks left, there is no coin, and "I eat you!" If the traveler picks right, "You get my troll's bag of gold!" But the bag is at the bottom of the river—the traveler sees it, finally, gleaming there. Traveler leaps in, tries to fish it out, but the treasure bag is made of air, illusion. It is only troll's gold. The troll leaps into the water and eats the traveler.

For what exactly was I offering Jeff, Bix, Frank, Will, Leah, Lizzie, Edwidge, Marla, and Glen in exchange for carrying my groceries and sometimes typing my query letters to magazines?

Jeff Dixon-Davidson, my first and best intern, got to see me up close and personal as I went about my business writing and producing a show that would run at The Kitchen, a, ahem, prestigious avant-garde arts space.

Some internships, I know, have consisted of less. Jeff typed some of my writing for the performances. He accompanied me to some meetings and helped me produce the show.

He also typed some of my free-lance magazine articles that had been commissioned by editors.

Somehow, I believed this was an unfair arrangement. In my mind, RSI had eaten up whatever writing ability I had had. And I believed it had eaten up my currency, my power to be published and taken seriously.

(Or had my leaving the *Voice* done that? Either way, my power was gone.)

In The Earthsea Trilogy, Ged, a powerful wizard, tells his young man not to bother going back for the magic staff Ged has left behind in the sand, about to be taken by the tide. (He and his companion have just journeyed into hell and saved the world.) But "leave it," he says to his buddy. "I spent all wizardry at that dry spring... I am no mage now."

I always really, really hated that part. What did it mean that Ged had "spent" his power? Was I just supposed to accept that?

I thought I had nothing left to give Jeff, a cheerful young guy who was into mass spaceflight and doll collecting. (He was smart, too, and the most conscientious intern I have had. He had a graduate degree in archaeology!) I felt I was trading him a stink bomb for his eggs and flowers.

With the other interns it was even worse. There was über-masculine Frank, an angry goy who taught young boys at a yeshiva and brought in essays about how much he hated their pale, weak, Jewish visages. I critiqued the essays for him, noting in my best neutral writing-teacher manner that "it was hard for me to feel very much empathy for the narrator."

I don't know if he got that. He did not last long in any case. Muscular Frank seemed resentful about hauling my groceries, despite my cripple's free writing advice.

Will was a former student of mine who applied for the internship when the Internet startup for which he worked folded. I came to dislike him more and more the more he worked for me. Yet he was always helpful, and occasionally kind—letting me know at a certain point that I did not have to pay him the $6 an hour, he wanted to help me anyway. So why did I dislike him so intensely? Was I afraid he saw me as a charity case? Will had a certain coldness to him. In his writing for our class, he had often put down people who didn't have much money to spend. He also mocked those men and women whose clothes and apartments weren't up to speed.

When I saw tall, gay, funny, slightly pudgy Will I felt ashamed to be poor and, I thought, on a downward slide in my life.

Strangely, as it seemed to me, Will was also applying to become an Episcopal priest. Reader, you may have guessed that my theological views were not at all in line with those of the Episcopal Church, but nonetheless it offended me somehow that Will, who wanted to be a priest, liked stylish clothes and enjoyed making fun of people who didn't buy them. Perhaps he was too human for my notion of a priest.

For our exchange, I helped him with his application to join the priesthood. Though, as I say, I understood that my own Gnostic views would necessarily be utterly different from Will's Episcopalian ones, I was deeply offended by the theology he evinced in his essays. Will, and, he claimed, the Episcopal Church, were of the opinion that priests were needed to intercede between God and the congregation. The idea was that regular people could not talk to God on their own. I hated that stupid idea! But reader, why should I have supposed that Will needed to have the same views about God as me, when I have never been an affiliant of organized religion, not even in my yeshiva days?

I detested him, I think, reader, because I detested myself. I think I could not bear that someone as human and fault-laden as Will wanted to help me.

With Edwidge the problem was simpler. She was a hard-working teacher with two jobs and three kids and the amazing residual energy to write a 500-page novel about public-school teachers who moonlighted as vigilante superheroes who hunted child molesters and put them through a set of retaliatory tortures.

I read her novel and critiqued it, which I considered a fair trade for her schlepping my bagels and taking out my trash.

Then one day Edwidge mentioned that she was in touch with what she called "some nice thugs" who occasionally supplied her with muscle when she had need of it. They had intervened—for free, just because they liked her and they were nice guys—when a corrupt principal needed to be shown the light. She had also utilized their services when she'd been having problems with her landlord.

I was fascinated with the unusual resources Edwidge had developed.

But, possessed of a most un-golem-like desire to preserve my own safety, I decided I did not want them around me. As soon as I believed unhazardously possible I told her I didn't really need an intern anymore, my situation had considerably improved.

She was very understanding.

Next there was Marla, a young lesbian who edited the weekly calendar for one of the city's gay papers.

For Marla, gentles, I feel a mix of guilt and rage—yes, I still feel them, seven years later. The interns I had who benefited the most from me were the ones who had a concrete piece of writing and wanted feedback on it. Marla was not one of these. Instead, she said, "The only thing I'd want from you is your ideas. But you'd probably wanna keep those to yourself, wouldn't you!"

My ideas?

Her request chilled me. There has always been a part of me with an old dwarf's suspicions about giving anything to younger people. They'll supplant me! They'll take everything I have! But somehow the way she put it particularly aroused my suspicions.

She seemed to believe, as I did, that her ideas would have to come from me or nowhere; as though we were in a zero-sum game where either Marla would steal all my apples and I would have none, or I would hold onto them and she would never get any. Somehow, neither of us imagined that there were other possible solutions. Teaching, for example—that I could help her develop her own ideas—or mutual development.

My suspicions weren't the only thing her request aroused. Marla was one of the most negative, caustic people I had met in a very long time, and it was horribly attractive, reader. Her saying "the only thing" she could possibly want from me were my ideas stirred my desire, reader, in a way I did not understand.

Because she did not want me, I wanted her. Specifically, I wanted her contempt—something I was getting anyway! In addition to no writing ideas, Marla had a scornful, lips-pursed manner that drew me like a set of iron filings to an enormous caustic magnet.

It sure was an odd dynamic between her and me. Marla, surly, physically strong, squat, making annoying jokes about sex and romance all the time (Her, in a Don Juan voice: "Want a date?" Me: "Uh, no, thanks!" Her, handing me a Medjool date from behind her back, triumphant: "I meant one of *these!*" She repeated this joke every time we shopped in the food coop.)

I could tell that Marla was not interested in me and for some reason this obsessed me, even though I found her very ugly and stumpy.

I was going to write that we were not at all on the same

wavelength. Except, unfortunately, actually I think we were. Marla was the sort of butch who, when you asked her why she wanted to date a certain woman, said, "Because she's got a great rack!"

Even in my butch days, I would never have said that. Still, I was known for saying provocative, inappropriate things that transgressed generally-agreed upon boundaries, all over the town. I was known, probably, as well for being lame and hard-to-take when I tried to date.

There was also the coincident fact that we were both resentful people. Once she knew I was not going to give her my ideas, Marla hated the fact that she was working for me, putting my milk away and filing my receipts. She would show up as agreed, but grimacing every time. Perhaps the last time I had her come to work for me was the day my mother died.

I did not know my mother was going to die that day, of course. It was a Sunday and I had arranged for surly, grumbly Marla to come over and help me with my taxes, which are hard to work out on your own with a hand injury. Even when I knew, in early morning, that my mother was dead I did not cancel Marla. Dully, I was thinking that I still had to finish my taxes, and I was worried that even on the day of my mother's death, if I put off tax-computing while I had an intern available, it surely would result in even more terrible disaster, like the IRS flying in through my closed window like a big black bestial bird of prey.

Or maybe I wanted to pretend that nothing had happened. This did not work very well, reader. After only ten minutes of looking at receipts with sour Marla, I sent her back home to Astoria.

The jig was up.

—Reader, I didn't plan to go into this now. Have I gotten ahead of myself? My mother's sickness was supposed to come in a discrete, well-ordered section that had nothing to do with my bad intern relations.

CHAPTER 11

My mother started to fade as soon as I did. Were we each other's simulacrum? Howsoever it happened, the day I had my first RSI doctor's evaluation was the last day my mother was ever capable of driving herself to the Long Island Rail Road station to pick me up for a visit.

I was supposed to come right after my appointment. I never did make it out that day to see her. My Mount Sinai exam wound up taking two hours longer than expected, and when I called to say how late I was, she told me to come back in a few days. She and her boyfriend, John, were already exhausted from just driving to the train.

Her lungs, propped up by magic all those years, failed gradually. She was only sixty-four when she started taking oxygen with her everywhere. Perhaps the year before she had started using a wheelchair sometimes—not because anything was wrong with her legs, but because her breathing was so poor it was hard for her to walk under her own power.

My mother had been complaining of ill health, you might say, ever since I had met her, but the reality seemed to have finally caught up to its promotion. Both she and I were supposed to have died during my birth, she said. "You almost died, and I almost died," she told me when I was four. "The hole was too small."

Our apocalyptic double murder-suicide was somehow averted by the hospital staff. Or perhaps by our own abilities as shamans. My mother and I have always known that we are incredibly gifted magicians, even at a time when one of us going through labor and the other was but a newborn.

Our bodies' link did not, of course, end there. My mother acquired her disability, the hole in her neck and the cutting-out of her voice box, at the age of thirty-six, and so did I acquire my own at thirty-six, a breaking of the hands that seemed almost ritual in its implication. (In *Diary of a Mad Housewife*, a novel I read as a child, Sue Kaufman writes about "thirty-sixitis," an alleged condition women get when they turn thirty-six—"a significant and dangerous age for a woman—like fifty for a man," one of her characters claims. It's the age at which Marilyn took her pills.)

Whenever my mother was angry because other people were not doing exactly what she wanted, she would shout in her hoarse caw-cry, "I'm a handicapped woman!" Of course, I did something like this, too, when it was my time to turn thirty-six.

What surprised me was how much it bothered me that I could not help her physically because my arms had broken. I was flabbergasted that I *wanted* to. I think I had never wanted to help her before.

Her physical state was shocking to me. For a while, she could still speak—my mother was one of the best practitioners in the world of esophageal speech, a method laryngectomees employed to talk—but she could no longer make me lunch, which she had liked to do when I'd come over. My mother loved to make me tuna fish sandwiches with tomato, and I had loved to eat them, reader, so we'd had moments and moments of her feeding me, of her nurturing me, when I'd come over to North Shore Towers, the famous old person's luxury co-op she lived in near Lake Success.

She didn't have enough steam to make a sandwich anymore, but she would get the nice young home health aide to buy me tropical fruit from the best market on the "arcade" level, mangoes, starfruit and papayas so that she would know

I was enjoying something special.

When she could no longer talk—when was this? The fall of 2000, after the spring in which my arms had broken?—she wrote notes for awhile when she had something especially important to communicate, like "Is *she* [the home health aide] the authority on the Q69 bus, or am?!"

When she could no longer write notes, she would just stare with her head raised grimly, looking like an American Indian warrior chief whose skin had inexplicably turned gray.

Years ago—twenty-one years ago to be absolutely precise—my mother had begun telling Josie, Aphra, and me that she was a devoted member of the Hemlock Society, the pro- assisted suicide group, and that she expected us to grind up twenty pills and slide them down her throat if necessary to help her die when her time came. (She didn't mention the pillow to smother her as a failsafe, but I later learned most Hemlock Society members requested that, too.)

But was I really supposed to do that? It was very hard to know. Certainly, she was experiencing horrendous pain. I eventually realized it was literally hurting her to breathe, and the doctors had given her a morphine patch as well as three different oral kinds of pain medication. There was an *ad libitum* morphine drip as well, for which my mother could press a button whenever she wanted a little extra.

She described her pain rather jauntily, though. "I feel what people feel like when they have cystic fibrosis," she would say triumphantly, "as though they're drowning!" And she would grin. "I *am* really drowning, little by little!"

While she was still speaking gleefully about her pain did not seem like a good time to kill her.

When she couldn't speak, though—and even the last couple of months she could—my mother sometimes looked really mortified and frustrated to be so helpless. I don't think I've told you what an industrious person my mother was, how she was always hatching book proposals, political campaigns against capitalism and homophobia, new ways of arranging the living room furniture, poems. Indeed, the year before she stopped being able to talk, my mother had written and published a kind of Cliff Notes guide to *Billy Budd*, put out two poetry chapbooks, and schemed each day to get gold and diamonds cheaply on eBay.

Now every two weeks it seemed she could do less and less. The nice young home health aide once a week, cleaning and buying fruit, had morphed into three distinct women who had the exhausting labor of taking care of her: the day woman, the night woman, and the woman who lived the entire weekend with her, my mother's home-health-aide version of the Maiden, the Mother, and the Crone, the threefold goddess who waxed and waned, washing my mother's buttocks and buying her Diet Coke, with the week.

My mother stopped being able to: make herself coffee, read books, read the newspaper, read her mail, do email, scramble an egg, take the cottage cheese out of the refrigerator so she could eat it, choose the presents she bought people for Christmas, even eventually—astounding!—watch TV.

My mother loved TV, and after she'd begun to get sick , she had actually descended as far as Judge Judy. Now she descended even further—no TV at all.

"You have to promise me," she'd demanded when I was fourteen, sixteen, twenty-three, thirty-two, "that you'll help me die." And, reader, I surely did promise, many times. It was hard not to promise my mother anything she wanted when I was a child. As I hurtled into my 20s, I promised again.

Was there ever a time when I refused to promise? I seem to remember one faintly, in my 30s. But is it a real memory? (Am I trying to find a light, bright period in which I either did *not* want to kill my mother or had the strength to resist saying I would be part of her death?)

Somehow, I thought the whole thing would be easy. As a child I even saw it as a matter of some moral urgency, reader. As someone who'd gotten hit regularly, I felt an affinity for anyone who wanted to escape their pain, even my mother.

Eventually, I had a sneaking suspicion that this might be a somewhat demanding request to make of one's child. But early on my promise was, at least in some respects, willing.

What in god's name were my responsibilities to her? It had always been hard to tell.

Whenever she made the request, my mother gave us to understand that she would always have the pills carefully stocked in the medicine cabinet to accomplish the task—"I've been putting them away," she would say slyly. "I always get some extra pills to put away." My mother had been threatening suicide off and on for years, so I absolutely believed that she had all the pills she needed, and that she maintained them constantly in a state of perfect readiness.

It was part of my belief in her all-comprehensive powers.

It was a shock when she turned out not to have the right kind of pills squirreled away. I know this is not the usual thing you read in the case of daughters caring for their ailing mothers. But, if she had ever had the pills, they had expired, lost their strength, been thrown away, or been taken for pleasure, in the moment. Also, it was now so long after the last time she had asked me that I could no longer be sure if my mother *wanted* to die.

She had asked me only when she wasn't sick and wasn't dying.

Now my mother had developed a hump of flesh in her back, and a stomach full of air like a malnourished child. Other parts of her body—her face, her back—looked skeletal. All my life, my mother had wanted me to feel sorry for her, but I never, ever had, until this stupid moment.

I tried to ask her once or twice, very, very quietly so the home health aide in the next room wouldn't hear. My mother was semi-silent by then, and when I whispered "Mom, do you want me to help you die? You have to tell me or I won't know," she said nothing.

I did do research at one point into getting the pills. I had a chemist girlfriend, bitter Betty Pill, who wrote me up a list of the combinations that I needed.

Was I going to be a murderer? It would have felt like a better role, I know, than being her victim, but from some mysterious place I found the strength to resist her request from long ago.

I felt so guilty. But I didn't want to do it if I wasn't sure she wanted me to. I also wanted to protect my own mind, from the torment of having killed my mother.

Lastly, I didn't want to go to jail. It wasn't worth it, perhaps even if she would have wanted me to do it. But I felt so selfish for putting my own shabby needs above hers.

It was horrible to me that for physical reasons, I couldn't give her even much more basic help than that. I was embarrassed and sad that I often could not reach to touch her, could not get her a glass of water or her sweater.

Here matters came to a head with one of the home health aides, Reyna, a motherly, middle-aged woman from Guyana who was my mother's favorite. Reyna was infuriated when I'd ask her to help me pour a drink for myself after my long, hot walk from the train, or to move a chair for me into the bedroom so I could sit with my mother and not have to sit on her bed.

She thought I wanted to make extra work for her.

"There is no problem with your arms," she told me, enunciating very clearly.

It was my mother's money—specifically, my mother's "long-term care" insurance, along with an extra mortgage on her co-op—that was paying for the home health aides. But my sister Josie had my mother's power of attorney and was the one who signed the checks, so Reyna decided it was not important to do what I wanted when I came, especially after Josie and I had our big falling out.

Let me backtrack for a moment, sweet pea. So many special powers are going up in flames in this sorry chapter that I must take you back to Brooklyn for a while, away from my mother's sad studio in Lake Success, towards my own one-bedroom in Park Slope, where I can no longer afford the neighborhood's luxe lifestyle and am putting my monthly food bills on my credit card with the hope that the balance will never come due.

Did I say "special powers"? Perhaps you have been wondering what has been keeping me alive all this time, at least in terms of rent and bottled water. It surely can't be the royalties from my book (for like most books, it does not earn back its advance), or my few freelance articles for Internet magazines, which I can only do a tiny amount of with voice software, and which pay lousy, anyway. It's not my mother or my savings (negative), but an even more magical bit of sustenance that I have curiously not written about before.

My grandparents on my father's side, the Minkowitzes from Russia, were members of the American Communist Party who at some point acquired shares in a fleabag hotel property on the Upper West Side.

I don't say "fleabag" to disparage; the entire history of my father and my father's side of the family has taught me not to disparage any of the smaller creatures often looked at with contempt, such as the flea.

When my father was alive, my parents were always daydreaming loudly about their future inheritance: how we'd all be rolling in dough when his parents died.

I didn't exactly believe it. My mother was always telling us stories about our eventual superhuman glory in all spheres of life, how we would light up the world and be the ones to rule it and be accounted the brightest individuals in the history of the universe.

Part of me believed her about this, it is true. But then she would say I was a piece of shit, and part of me believed that, too.

Hearing my mother and my usually silent father crow about how we, the Minkowitzes on welfare in the roachy apartment, would be rich someday, seemed as untenable a prospect as the idea that my original name had been Kal-El and I was Superman's cousin.

"Rich" was relative then. My father's dream in the '70s was to open an Orange Julius, which was like a Papaya King except a little cheaper and more seedy. An Orange Julius might have been where a street side drug dealer and a corrupt cop went to enjoy an orange slushy together, or where poor kids would quench their parched throats after blackout looting.

I pitied my father, especially when I was a child, that the furthest he could dream was an Orange Julius. My mother had instilled in us that art, literature, and philosophy were the only things that counted, that it was vaguely dirty to have a store of any kind.

Never mind that my father, the potato-chip salesman and massage parlor-promoter, was the one working to pay for our tickets to hear Ntozake Shange and Adrienne Rich.

He *was* silent. All I really remember him saying to me is "*Farbissiner hint!* ["Nasty dog!" in Yiddish], and "Piece of shit!"

Other than that, I seldom heard his voice, except for when he sang nonsense syllables like "chitty, chitty, be, chitty bam" and "bitty bam, bitty bam." Until I was in my 30s and my father was long gone, I didn't know these nonsense chants were part of a venerable Jewish tradition. I had read about something called a "word salad" in the psychology books Josie brought home and thought my father was just intoning those syllables because he was crazy.

I didn't know that they were actually *nigunim*, holy Hasidic chants that Jews from the Ukraine and Poland had been singing since the Baal Shem Tov.

How was I stripped of anything connecting my father to what was holy?

I don't even know whether my father's family was Hasidic, in the distant past or even recently. (We always assumed his parents had never been religious, just because they were Communists). But the only book I ever saw my father read, after all, was *My Name Is Asher Lev*, about a

162

young artist in a Hasidic family.

(Was he an artist? He had written a song and copyrighted it in his 20s. My mother was always making him sing it to us so we could all make fun of him for it: "In the spring, the flowers bloom," in his sincere baritone, "Young lovers everywhere..." Maybe like a little-boy offspring of Sinatra and Johnny Mercer.

How could I have ridiculed that song? I prize it now.)

So what did my father's slightly nasal, somewhat feminine baritone say, those two or three times, about our eventual windfall? "See, Biggie," he would say to me smiling, "We're gonna be rich. I'm gonna open that Orange Julius."

— How I remember, with a shock, that he did speak to me affectionately sometimes. He called me "Biggie" and "Butch." Reader, I had never heard the word "butch" before and had no idea that he might have meant it disparagingly. I kind of liked it when he used those names, though I always found his affection hard to reconcile. Mostly, what I associated with him was painful punches, so when he'd look at me and say "Butch!" fondly, I would feel a mental disconnect. When he'd put his arm around me when we were sitting in the front seat of the car together, it was even worse. I think he may have meant it affectionately, but I was afraid of him physically, and I worried on some unthinking level that he might squeeze until I croaked in pain.

What else?

When I was four or five, he warned me against putting my fingers inside the grille of a room fan. I could tell he was agitated and upset at the thought. "My parents told me not to," he said, "but I put my fingers inside a fan when I was little and I got hurt!"

In retrospect, I value his warning so much. Because it was one of the only times he ever tried to protect me.

He gave me one other piece of fatherly advice, when I was fifteen. I had just come out (as bisexual, incidentally, not gay), and my father wanted to tell me sincerely that he thought it'd be bad for me. "Donna, your mother and I have a great sex life! I'd be sad to know you were missing out on that!"

I'm still horrified he brought up their great sex life, and angry that he didn't want me to be gay. (Also annoyed that he failed to notice I liked men, too.) But it was also one of two things he ever said to me that a protective guardian might say, reader, so I also kind of treasure it.

Later when he was white and skinny from cancer, he wept when I said goodbye to him at the Amtrak station, going back to Yale. It was the last time I ever saw him, and it was important. (Thanks, Dad.)

My father's mother, Shirley, died a month after he did, which meant Josie, Aphra, and I inherited directly from her. She had stayed largely unvisited in a nursing home for nine years, after my mother had literally sent her packing from our Co-op City apartment. (She'd pushed Shirley out into the hallway, then tossed her packed suitcase right behind her. I was there and I saw. Finally, my mother's threat to pack somebody's suitcase had been made good on!)

Shirley had lived with us for only a few months, after Daddy's father died in 1973. It was in the middle of my family's worst time, I know—my mother's larynx had been removed only a little more than a year before, and my father had started hurting me. I moved onto the yellow loveseat in the living room so that Shirley could have my room, and on that loveseat I began to stay up all night.

I was terrified of what I might dream if I let myself sleep. For the first time, I was afraid of vampires, werewolves, and grinning skeletons, and terrified that if I was dreaming I would think they were real. I numbed myself out with TV every night so that I wouldn't sleep.

When Shirley moved out, I stayed on in the living room. Claimed to like it. Let Josie have my old room. (Shortly after she threw her out, my mother pretended to "relent" enough to drive Shirley to the nursing home.)

When my father's mother was dead, and Daddy, too, Aphra, Josie, my mother, and I went to meet the lawyer who was the executor of her will. The lawyer—and my mother, too—emphatically urged my sisters and me to endow my mother with her own slice of our inheritance. (For surprisingly, Shirley had not left her anything.) My sisters and I were twenty-three, twenty-two, and eighteen, and we did give my mom her cut, of course.

Afterwards, the four of us were gleeful. We went out to a more expensive lunch then any of us had ever had before—glorious baby lettuces, cold poached WASPy salmon. The lawyer's office was in Rockefeller Center—even more glorious!—and we ate in a cafe overlooking the golden statue of Atlas there.

The money: in the beginning it was only $400 a month, but it *was* free money, reader, and as such had a curious odor of adventure and freedom associated with it.

It was my freshman year in college, and the first thing I bought was a black leather jacket ($90). I had always, always, always wanted one.

A woman I was in love with at Yale said of the jacket, "Delicacy, elegance—and shoulders!"

I didn't buy much else with the money until four or five years later. I was working at the Columbia University law library, a job that made me feel like Bartleby the scrivener. I was the Bindery Assistant, meaning I was supposed to send periodicals to get bound with other issues of the same periodical, and in an appropriate color. (I made all the Marxist law journals red.) I had a part-time, work-study graduate student who was supposed to help me carry the books, a man who was older than me and would stand much too close to me in the desolate Bindery Elevator and smile broadly. I could not think of what to do about it because the grad student was from Africa and I was officially in a position of power over him.

But I left after six months so I could try to write for the

Voice, where I had sold a few pieces already. I took a half-time job as a receptionist at the NOW Legal Defense and Education Fund, then I ditched it for a quarter-time job answering the phones at a female executives' group so I could write more.

Eventually, I did not need to have a day job at all.

Are you hating me already, reader? Bear in mind that I have always hated rich people, too. And I did struggle with an obligation I then felt to hate myself. (Also I felt a duty to "earn my keep," because those who earn passively from stocks are supported by the rest of society that works. That was one of the reasons I became a radical journalist.)

But in fact I had not become independently wealthy so much as independently working-class. (For my *Voice* income by itself paid for my Kmart wardrobe of butch T-shirts and that was about it.) But then, as real estate prices began their inexorable rise in Manhattan, I gradually became independently middle-class.

Another special power I can elucidate further here—when my father hit that sergeant and got put in the U.S. Army stockade, my mother, who told the story to us, said that he had "gone berserk." *Berserk* means "bear shirt," I have just found out. Reader, I was actually *right* when I said that he had been bear baited! That was just a lucky guess! (Exactly what William Blake had in mind when he said, "What is now proved was once only imagined.") In the Norse sagas, *berserkers* were men who wore bearskins and became like the bear, crazy with rage, striking trees, boulders, and their own families and friends as well as the enemy. Some of them may well have been historical men in whom their kings deliberately induced this rage.

They were very good at frightening people, which is why the kings kept them around.

Berserkers thought they were impervious to wounds, because they could not feel them in their mad state.

Sometimes they took off their shirts and went naked into

battle, because they were so sure they could not be hurt.

My father might just as well have been the original golem. The men in the bear shirts had superhuman strength as long as the fit was on them, but afterwards grew much weaker than ordinary men and women.

They were very easy to control then. They also grew ashamed.

Coincidentally—no lie!—for many years I had thought of my father as a wounded bear, trapped in a net of humiliations and goaded so that he would rear on his hind legs, and dance.

That net became his major point of connection with my mother; whenever she touched it they both were spellbound.

CHAPTER 12

Now my mother began to grow weaker, smaller, and easier to put in a cage, too, if anyone had wanted to—like the bear-men when their fits had left them. It was painful for me.

I was surprised how awful it was the year she forgot my birthday. She had always gone all out for my birthday.

I told you, my mom had always thought I was a special one.

Sometimes I hated it: There was the year she hired the Yale Precision Marching Band to play for me, as a surprise, in the dorm common room when everyone was watching. I did love it the time in high school when she made an arrangement with an inexpensive florist to get me flowers every month for the whole year. That was amazing—one of the best gifts I've ever received from anyone. There were some ruby and diamond rings that made me feel like a whore, but also novels that got me interested in science fiction for the first time (*Out of the Silent Planet, The Left Hand of Darkness*, a picture-book about Poseidon).

What does it mean to lose your source of power?

I was lonely, even as I was trying not to demand from my friends what I had always demanded: that they take away my unhappiness immediately, as my mother's Jane had done for her. I tried not to call people when I felt desperate, even though I almost always felt desperate. I tried to remember that my friend Eileen had children and they weren't me.

Eileen was a really good mother, and I would have liked so much to be her child. Her children, Alma and Manny, always got to be as sad or angry or happy as they were.

I kept wanting Olive, my newish therapist, to tell me I was doing a good job, but she wouldn't do it. "That sounds maybe like something maternal," the therapist said, "and that is not a role that I should fill."

Shit. I thought that was supposed to be the *very purpose* of a therapist?

I would take the long, cold express-bus ride out to Queens every week or so, where I would recite poetry to my real mother and sing old songs to her.

Out of the night that covers me
Black as the pit from pole to pole...
I am the master of my fate
I am the captain of my soul

("Invictus" was my mother's all-time favorite poem.)

Although I might not have a very present mother, I had the uncanny sensation that I myself had a child now—my Repetitive Strain Injury. It was as though I had carefully nurtured and birthed this condition, and I was now required to take care of it. I felt much more responsibility than I ever had before, for this bizarre RSI baby. What did it look like, my baby? Did it have craggy folds to its face, like a poltergeist? Was it prickly and rough-skinned and purple, one of those infants that looks like a cactus pear? I only knew that I had to take care of it. I dreamed it was sweet and warm, and that I had to learn to hold it as though it were a tiny baby, not a sack of potatoes. In the dream I carried it off my wrist in a little plastic Rite Aid bag at first, unsupported and unprotected.

My personal delicate-little-fairy routine seemed for the first time to be growing old. For one thing, it was much harder to pay the rent than it had ever been. My health expenses were high, and my income from the hotel failed to cover them, reader. I

169

was shamed by this, and also by the fact that writing fast enough to work myself with magazine work seemed to be too dangerous for me now, even with my special disability software.

Clearly, I had been a rampant failure at preparing myself for times like these. Wordsworth, who was once my own favorite poet, would wonder every now and then why he expected other people to "Build for him, sow for him, and at his call/ Love him, who for himself will take no heed at all?"

I expected other people to always spot me, too.

All the time.

I'd often thought of Wordsworth's statement of nonchalant dependence on others, because golems are taught never to take any heed for ourselves, either. We are taught to jump in the sea and drown, to smother fires with our own bodies. We run into walls if the rabbi says to. The rabbis do take care of our basic bodily needs, but it is actually unclear whether golems have any. (That we are under the rabbis' *authority* is not in dispute.) There was a way that my unearned income from my Russian grandparents' property had helped keep me a child, which is to say a golem; "an unformed thing"; "an embryo." In present-day Hebrew, the most common meaning for golem is "cocoon." But was it a cocoon that smothered or that fed?

Now I had to use every card in my hand, and so, like the good bullshit artist I am, I vigorously used all my credit cards. Banks kept offering me even more of them! I taught three of my writing classes at once, and looked into writing gay male porn for a website owned by a friend of Andy's. In the porno, I tried to turn Betty Pill, a Chinese-American, into a hulking, dominant, sulky Asian man, which I thought would appeal to all the non-Asian boys. "Ralph Wu glared at me. 'Get down on the floor.'" The pieces remained too literary.

I traded writing classes to a poor student in exchange for taking out my garbage. I had lunch with my old editor at *The Nation*, trying to scare up work. I tried to manage doing freelance pieces like the one she actually gave me on the new, boring anti-gay ballot measure in Florida, while still protecting my arms (they got flared up, and *The Nation* most unfeelingly declined to give me a cover line.) I lunched with a boy I'd had a crush on in high school, who was now dean of a liberal rabbinical college, where I unsuccessfully lobbied to teach creative writing. An old ACT UP buddy of mine was starting to edit a magazine for people with breathing problems? Great! I let him take me out to a succulent lobster dinner and wrote a venomous screed about how much I hated smokers.

Perhaps slowly, slowly, slowly, like a tree growing from a tiny acorn under time-lapse photography, my arms began to get better. "Little by little, step by step," Dr. Sing used to say to me confidently, several times a year. Everyone else seemed impatient with the excessively languid pace at which my RSI was improving.

Strangely, I was less impatient. For myself, I had decided that getting better from RSI was half my job. The other half was writing. As long as I could advance along both paths, I was making progress.

I did notice that some point, I had stopped being in pain all the time. Dr. Mayhew attributed this to my judicious refusal to do all the things that were bad for my hands. And I did spend least half my time doing work to save my strange little baby. Acupuncture, physical therapy, biweekly massage, swimming, sessions with an "ergonomist" who figured out how tall my desk should be. Most of my money now, too, seemed to go for the care of the ghostly creature inside me.

This was the same few months, reader, that my mother began to get as if magically worse. Do you know the William Blake poem in which a very young man and a very old woman take turns binding each other down upon rocks? They bind each other down for their "delight," and also to feed off each other. "She lives upon his shrieks & cries, and she grows young as he grows old." Had I allowed my mother become a kind of voodoo doll for me? Did her decline make me grow?

My mother wrote a poem I found unbearable around this

time, called "Never-Ending Stories." It was about, er, how horrible it is to keep living when you're in pain. I had to hear it many, many times, because the visiting music therapist from Cabrini Hospice was often in my mother's apartment when I came by, setting my mother's poems to music.

Sarah, the nice young music therapist, had seized on this particular poem, and she would sing it whenever I visited. (My mother, no longer able to talk, would nonetheless avidly conduct, a skill she had learned at Hunter College High School, the school for the gifted I had gone to, too, where every student is required to learn how to do this in the first-year music class.)

Never-Ending Stories

In my house are passages,
hideaways,
and corners,
one door leads to another,
and another,
and another...
In my house I hear sweet music
coming from the walls,
angels hover in the attic
singing Hallelujah praises.

I am bleeding,
I am falling,
life is measured out in hours
'though the moments last forever.

I see through darkened windows
Morning's reprisal,
each new day deposing
another,
and another...

I was confused by the fact that, now that my mother was getting weaker and sicker and therefore had much less capacity to hurt me, she seemed to be trying to avoid the behavior that had hurt me in the past.

For example, she finally seemed to have noticed (or perhaps, to care) that I did not want her to get undressed in front of me, which I'd been telling her with urgency for years.

Now that I did not mind her taking off her clothes when she was uncomfortable because she was so ill and it was hard for her to move around, now she finally wanted to protect me from it. She had the home health aide hold up a sheet just for me.

It was similar with the commode, which she kept near her bed so she would not have to walk the few extra feet to the bathroom. Now that she was ill enough that it seemed quite practical and understandable that she would sometimes go in front of us, she would gesture to me (but no other family members) to leave the room so that my delicate sensibilities would no longer have to be offended by seeing my mother on the toilet.

When she could still talk, my mother said to me once, "I would really like to see you more often." This was at a time when I was seeing her once every week or two. When I replied I was honest but also not overly tender: "I see you *as much as I can see you,* Mom. This is as much as I can see you." Even at death's door, even moderating herself, my mother was still too frightening to visit more than once a week.

I felt guilty that I couldn't see her more. My sister Josie was furious that I couldn't. In our distinctly different golem socializations, poor Josie had been the more conventional of us by far. She had become the best servant in the family, like a sort of preternaturally perspicacious butler.

It surprised me how she turned out, because when we were kids she was the scrappiest one. She actually fought back against my mom so forcefully when we were small that my mother put Josie into little girls'-therapy, where I never had to be sent. Josie actually got mad, screamed at Mommy, slammed doors and tore off down the street.

But when we were grown, it was Josie who ached to be a good daughter.

Not me. I myself hated the word "good," and I cringed when I thought about how disgustingly good I had been through the years.

Josie became, as they say, my mother's primary caregiver. She hung out all weekend long with my mother, every weekend, and usually several nights during the week, especially when my mother was finding it especially hard to breathe. Josie had become a sort of Mr. Fix-It for my mother, whether it came to her oxygen hookup or the picture on her TV, like a replacement for my father in all his two-sided grandeur. Josie, the only straight woman amongst the daughters, had become the butchest of us all. She had long been the handiest one with a power screwdriver and a saw, and the only one who enjoyed rousting the young hoodlums who were trying to steal her car. "What the fuck do you think you're doing?" she would say to them laughing, belligerent, happy to have caught them in the act. "Get away from my car!"

Pure aggression gleamed in Josie's muscles and smiled in her fat. She was a curiously ambiguous figure, and still occasionally bullied my mother and snapped at her, just as often as she was a helpful servant. Josie is the most changeable being I have ever known, and I have always felt ambivalent about her. Our relationship seesawed wildly. One week we would be on the outs, and the next almost in love.

She loved to give embraces, though they were not always nice ones. She was like the 8 year-old boy who enjoys giving wet kisses to all the other children on the playground, and then punching them hard and pulling them under the sprinkler. (Then the boy wipes his snot on them.) When I adored Josie, I would ignore the violence seeping out of her like coffee from a leaky paper bag and treat her like Clifford or Big Bird, a polymorphously perverse big cuddly hunk o' love and warm support and steadfastness.

And she was that, too. When I've been close to her it's been the most wonderful thing that ever happened to me, it's like having a lover right up against you with no conflict or difference whatsoever for three million years. It's like dating Barney, warmer than anything. She just switches back and forth, that's the problem.

Aggression vacillated with icky-softness in my sister, as though she were a giant jellyfish. Perhaps it was merely a consequence of being a golem, because our kind must always vacillate in some way between softness and attack. But Josie clung to those poles more obviously than most—much more obviously than me, for instance. She had made collages of Looney Tunes characters that I found terrifying. Daffy Duck and Porky Pig smiled at the viewer maniacally, and Yosemite Sam sneered happily as though he were about to crush a gnat in his humongous hands. Next to them on her wall were giant photos of kittens and babies I found just as frightening. Josie's sweetness, when present, was so cloying that it was hard for me to ever find it authentic—although now I wonder. Perhaps she was simply a person cut in half.

She liked to ask me, during those interludes when we spoke every night, what I had just had for dinner. "Tun-y fish?" For of course she liked to talk in baby-talk to me. "Want some sod-y? Want to take a drive-y in the car-ry?" Even when we were "being close," the baby-talk repelled me, and I would try to change the subject. "Duney," she would say, calling me by one of my family nicknames from childhood, "don't you love it when you make a nice big fart and it smells so good?" Or she would describe the nice big doody she had made. Even when Josie was being pleasant she always felt too intimate to me, as though she were trying to burrow into my colon.

But I, of course, felt wildly flattered sometimes anyhow

175

when she wanted to be nicely in my colon. For golems, having anyone come that close is rare, sweet reader.

I saw love, most of the time, as something that could shift back and forth, on a dime, between sweetish conversation and anal rape. It had always been that way for me, except with Aphra, and she'd left home early.

Yet sometimes Josie was genuinely compassionate to me.

When I was a little kid she was kind enough to take me with her to her junior-high-school friends' houses—for I never had friends of my own until I was twelve. Once when I was nine, she actually frightened off a would-be child molester trying to make friends with me in McDonald's. I was eating a burger, by myself, when my sister turned up and spoke harshly to the man who was chatting me up in the most flattering way. I'll never forget how annoyed I was at the time, but I am quite sure she saved me. A couple years later, when I got my period the first time, my mom was several hundred blocks uptown at Columbia grad school, so it was Josie who showed me how to use sanitary napkins (they were the old kind, without adhesive, that you really had to be taught how to use). And for years after my mother went back to college, it was Josie, in middle school, who used to make dinner for herself and me every night by combining Campbell's Tomato Rice Soup and Campbell's Stewed Tomatoes. I felt the love in that. It was so much better to eat them together, as food that somebody had combined with intention, and partly to take care of me.

Still, I'd always seen Josie as a member of the same species as my parents. She was someone who threatened often to hit me, just like they did. And she *did* hit me sometimes. Because they all had black or nearly-black hair, I believed for a long time that if only I had black hair, too, I would become a powerful person like my mother and father and sister, able to get angry, and to get whatever I wanted from other people.

(Early on in my RSI journey I did dye my hair black for a

little while, reader. I was thinking that my recently dyed blonde hair was maybe an all-too-disgusting and obvious sign of my good girlness—or fairyness—whatever it was that had made me unprotected and injured. It didn't work though. All I got was one of my writing students commenting, "Nice Goth look!")

When I was twenty-seven, though, Josie had suddenly gotten a very serious health problem. I was jolted to realize that even my dangerous sister wasn't impenetrable. I was shaken, and made a special effort from then on to never notice the bad parts.

In high school Josie, a compulsive eater, had used to put a heavy chain on the refrigerator at night with a lock only she possessed the key to. She put a lock on so she wouldn't devour everything in the middle of the night. This meant that I couldn't get a soda from the fridge when I was thirsty, but Josie would break her own lock so she could eat the contents of the refrigerator. At the time I felt like I was living with a dangerous beast that needed to be restrained but could break every restraint put on it.

So I teeter-tottered for years between these perspectives. Josie would kiss me sweetly and then suddenly come out with, "When you were little you had such a bad speech impediment that you sounded really stupid. We all laughed at you."

Every now and again I would ask Josie if she'd be willing to talk about our relationship. Her response had always been the same: "I don't have time for that!"

Is it "Brownian motion" in physics where dust particles suddenly move one way, then another? And the stream of dust keeps going back and forth, maddeningly and endlessly. This motion, on my part at least, finally came to an end a year and a half after RSI had started to change how I related to other people.

It was September—precisely, it was September 2001. It had been a difficult summer. I had bad asthma attacks from allergic reactions to all the mosquito bites I got walking in the dank Ravine at Prospect Park, my attempt at a staycation. My oven emitted noxious fumes, and my landlord refused to fix it.

I could not go away because Josie had announced that she was going away to a weight-loss program at a spa in Sedona for the whole summer. "I'd like you to stay in Brooklyn for all of July and August," she said, so that one of us would constantly be on hand if Mommy had any problems.

Whether I went or not, the three home health aides would be with her around the clock the whole time.

Also, the trip I wanted to take would have been a very close one, to the Hudson Valley, two hours away. But Josie wanted me to stay in the five boroughs. I was feeling guilty that she took so much more assiduous care of my mother than I did, so I agreed.

I had only enough money to go away for two nights anyhow, though I had yearned to spend those two nights away in July or August—when everyone else in the sweltering city was gone.

I didn't go. I saw my mom every week in July and August. She was not doing particularly well. She could still talk, but barely, and seemed quite absent, I believe from the morphine.

I arranged to take my two-night vacation in September, when Josie would be back and be able once again to supervise my mother constantly.

When Josie returned from the spa, I did voice some frustration to her. And I made a request: "Please don't make plans for staying away the whole summer again without asking me about my plans, if you'd like me to stay in the city during that time."

Josie grumbled, "Donna, Donna, Donna, you don't know when to fucking shut up."

Then, right before I was to go to Mohonk, September 11 happened. Reader, everyone in New York City, including me, was traumatized. The office where I now got physical therapy was only a block away from the World Trade Center, and I had sometimes ducked into the towers just to buy a soda in the mornings. Afterwards, there was an enormous evil-smelling, dark-gray cloud in the sky over Brooklyn for months from the things and the people that had been burnt. I am not exaggerating about how long it lasted— it was months, reader. For a day or two, I wore a surgical mask so that I wouldn't have to breathe the choking smoke. I tried going to the physical therapy office, which the owner, Winston Carroll, LPT, assured me was absolutely safe, but the air was so much worse in the financial district that I decided to switch to Winston's uptown facility, 130 blocks away at the other end of Manhattan. Afterwards, it came out that many persons eventually died just from breathing the air around the first office, and that Christie Whitman, head of the EPA, had lied to the public when she said it was safe to breathe on Vesey Street.

After September 11, I felt like I needed even more intensely to go someplace green, and I was actually glad that I had postponed my summer vacation till the following week, when I would take the bus to New Paltz and hike in the mountains. I pedal-boated in Lake Mohonk and was startled to find I was strong enough to steer a boat. Then, swimming on my back in the water with my trusty aqua-jogger around me to support my arms, suddenly I felt the Lady and Lord of the Lake holding me up, heard them whispering affection. Please just go with me here: the Lord and Lady are the powers that protect the trees, keep the water as pure as they can, and try to hold everyone who falls in. They held me, both of them, this time, and I felt their big, delicate damp fingers on my face, like a poppy.

When I got back to the city, Josie, my mother and I all went out to brunch together at a glitzy Long Island restaurant. I'd been trying not to see them together, for they were worse as a pair. With my mom these days, Josie acted like a husband who's obeyed his wife so punctiliously for so long that he wants to smack her. (The Josie-husband wanted to smack me too, feeling I'd gotten off scot-free from all the work he was stuck with.)

But Josie and my mother both liked—if, that is, my mother still "liked" anything—going out all three of us to brunch together, like they thought American families were supposed to. I told you Josie was conventional in her outward preferences; even my mother, the old lefty, shocked me on this day by wearing an American flag lapel pin because of the attack.

I came in the car with them. I am the only non-driver in the family, reader—not just because of my arm injury, but because of, perhaps, my essence.

For years, I had been stuck in cars with either Josie or my mother as they either screamed abuse at me or insisted on taking me someplace I did not want to go.

Now, I had gone in the Pinto with them to this schlocky, overgilt restaurant in Nassau, far from any bus or train. There were dying chrysanthemums in a big vase; there was frozen shrimp for the price of fresh. Josie pushed my mom in her wheelchair inside; I held the door. Josie made a sour scowl at me because I myself couldn't push my mother's wheelchair forward by as much as an inch. In the car, Josie had made a face whenever I had spoken.

My mother could only use her poor weak lungs to utter about four words per hour, but we all ordered brunch, affecting to be cheery. I got the jumbo shrimp, which unfortunately were too large for me to pick up without serious hand pain. I wanted to ask Josie to help me cut or lift them, but didn't because it would annoy her. So I changed the subject to a more neutral topic.

"He didn't mean to kill them!" my sister said. "They only got killed by accident!"

We were debating about George Bush, who had just bombed Afghanistan, accidentally killing thousands of civilians.

Josie and I seldom argued about politics—for indeed, she

was a moderate-liberal, a right-winger only in the context of my family which spanned from left to ultra-left. (When she'd unexpectedly had to deal with homeless addicts as part of a job, however, she did have the unfortunate habit of referring to them as "subhuman pieces of shit.")

I said, "It doesn't matter if he didn't intend to kill them! He did kill them!"

Tension was lingering in both of us from the summer, and 9-11 had made us even edgier than usual. Both of us were avid for a fight, the same way 9-11 had made all of us New Yorkers want to stuff ourselves senseless with food and drink and fuck until our heads came off.

Josie said, "But he's like Hitler!" referring to Osama bin Laden.

I said, "But we already killed 3,000 people, more than died on 9-11!" We fought about the war, over my shrimp and Josie's crab-stuffed flounder. (Both of them were in fact delicious, reader.) Though we were actually mad at each other, it was also rather fun to fight that day, and we let it loose much more freely than we usually did.

Then we got on the subject of my two nights at Mohonk.

I said how much I loved it, how healing it had been for me to swim in the lake.

"How much did it cost?" asked Josie, not quite casually.

I blinked briefly, trying to find the question noninvasive. Then I smiled, thinking my hesitancy must be my own fault. My old therapist, Edna, had taught me to interpret all the feelings of fear I felt in Josie's presence as mere symptoms of my inability to love.

I laughed, putting it all on me. "I'm a little afraid to tell you," I chortled at myself, "because for some reason I have a fantasy that you might judge me," and I giggled at myself, making clear that I considered this fantasy one of the silliest I had ever conceived in my silly little brain.

But, "You're right, I do judge you!" Josie said stone-faced. "Tell me how much you spent!"

Low.

I was shocked. The same way, reader, I had always been shocked whenever Josie started pushing me around. Regardless of the circumstances, I always, always reverted to assuming Josie was going to be loving and kind with me. Golemhood for me had sometimes amounted to a curious innocence, like a caul that covered my eyes and nose and ears.

My sister and my mother had been asking me how much I spent on things for years, just as they always wanted to know other intimate details. Now I chuckled nervously. "It's kind of personal," I said. "I'd rather not tell you."

Josie exploded. "I can go to the Internet myself and see how much you spent if you don't tell me!"

Actually, she couldn't. Mohonk Mountain House, the admittedly expensive, quite odd 19th-century Quaker lodge where I had gone, had occasional great bargain offers, one of which I had seized on.

But why did she think she had a right to know, in any case?

Josie shouted, "People who borrow money shouldn't go on vacation!"

I had, because my treatment cost so much, borrowed $500 from Josie at the beginning of the summer, with an agreement to pay it back in October, when Salon would pay me that much for a book review. It was now September 29.

"But we agreed that I'd pay you back in October! It's not October yet!"

"People who borrow money from others shouldn't go on vacation!" she repeated loudly across the table. Josie earned about $135,000 a year, which included her work income as a real estate agent plus the dividends from our hotel property. I earned $35,000.

My mother ate her scrambled eggs slowly, keeping her eyes down.

"You know what a horrible year I had. And I only went away for two nights. You went away for two months. You're saying I didn't deserve to go on vacation?"

"No!" my sister shouted triumphantly.

I wanted to clarify further. "You're saying I don't deserve to go on vacation??"

"No, you don't!" Josie said with considerable satisfaction, as she grandly stalked off to go to the bathroom.

Now I did what I had never done before. I left. Even though I didn't have a car. I said goodbye to my mother and I asked the maître d' to call a taxi for me. She was very gracious about it.

The cab to the nearest Long Island Rail Road station cost about forty bucks, but I did not mind handing the driver the two prodigiously fresh, newly minted 20s I had for some reason garnered from the ATM that morning. Though I was hurting for money, it was worth it.

My relationship with the other oldest living golem of all time changed forever then. Reader, I ended it.

CHAPTER 13

I felt alone, though. Josie had been good for a conversation after work, for cooing noises on the phone.

I went to Prospect Park and saw the places we had gone together in the past ten years: the lake, the beautiful boathouse, the sprawling hedgerows on the eastern side of the park, not far from the skating rink. We had had picnics. She often used to say to me encouragingly, "You're a good person!" (she used to say "You're nothing but a piece of shit!" just as often).

The previous May, on my birthday, Josie and bitter Betty Pill had taken me out to a fancy restaurant together. I'd had the rack of lamb and chocolate soufflé. Betty Pill had broken up with me the following month, an act for which I was extremely grateful. I hadn't even been attracted to poor Betty, who wore button-down clothes and sensible lipstick. I'd dated her because she seemed as sweet and unthreatening as Elmo, but the girl had had a mean streak like a straight razor.

I felt lonely, snooping around the Oriental Pavilion in Prospect Park, sword-dancing with my sister's ghost on the colored, polished tiles. Right over here we had seen the ducks, and there, one day, we had gone to the zoo. Reader, I was finally done with being shocked. I had lost a kind of virginity around my awareness of maltreatment. I didn't think I would ever be able to become unenlightened again. It was a mind-blowing gift.

That caul or hymen was gone forever. In Gnosticism, the gnosis that is achieved is perhaps best translated as "becoming fully acquainted" or "deep familiarity." It is an act of joyous reception, whether or not the thing one is finally becoming familiar with is good or bad. "Every act of becoming conscious," Adrienne Rich wrote about this spirited transformative process, "is an unnatural act."

In Gnosticism, eating of the tree of knowledge of good and evil was a *good* thing. The serpent encouraged us to do it because he was on our side. I could not believe that I had allowed Josie to be such a destructive presence in my life for so long. But I felt powerful because I had cut her, finally, from that precious place.

Soon she left a message on my answering machine in baby-talk, sing-songing, "Duney, let's let bygones be bygones!" I told her I wanted to do something different. "Let's talk about our relationship and work on it seriously together." Josie yelped, "I don't have time for that!" She wanted to be "friends" again but only if we stayed blind and deaf and numb, and quite silent.

She also inquired, with not a little resentment, "How did you get away from the restaurant?"

My mother had to go to Cabrini Hospice in Manhattan for a month that fall—much more convenient for me (if not for my mom) because it was easy to get to by subway. I also liked Cabrini because it had kind volunteers and staffers who didn't mind setting up a chair for me or putting things where I could reach them, unlike my mother's main home health aide.

My mother sometimes tried to wrestle her clothes off at Cabrini—I think she felt overheated—and the staff folksinger, who strolled around with a guitar and took requests, thought he was being kind by refusing to let her strip and smoothing her pajamas back down again. I argued with him—I thought she should be allowed to wear or not wear whatever made her physically comfortable—but it was a battle I could not win and I decided to focus on other necessary struggles like making sure she got her meds and showing up for my mother even at those times when I'd miscalculated and Josie was already there.

For the baby-talk had turned definitively back to abuse: when I was sitting on the edge of my mother's bed, stroking her hair, Josie came right up to the edge of my body and said, "Move."

I said, "Usually, people say 'excuse me' in circumstances like this when they want to be nice."

Josie said, "I don't want to be nice."

My mother died six months later, surprising us all who had expected her to die at least two years previous.

Four days before, I'd visited—mom was back home again in Great Neck—and had a run-in with the chief home health aide.

"You have no problem with your hands," Reyna said again to me (my mother loved her), "you just want me to carry chairs and work for you all day long. But you're not paying my salary! Josie's paying my salary!"

Reyna was overjoyed to have intuited that my sister and I were no longer friends.

My dams burst. "What exactly is your problem? I'm just trying to visit my mother and I have a disability, and I don't always want to have to sit on her bed!"

My mother, for a change, grew quite alert from our shouting—looked very alarmed, actually—hoisting her head and shoulders up from the bed and gazing at both of us. I felt guilty when she died a few days later, as though my shouting had pushed her over the edge and made her feel finally unwelcome in her own apartment.

How I would like to avoid telling you about the funeral. Josie called me in the morning to let me know my mother had expired in the small hours. Without consulting Aphra or me, Josie had immediately sent my mom into the mortuary assembly-line and ordered a funeral like a pizza for the next day.

"Can't we wait a couple of days?" I asked.

"No!"

She'd planned all the particulars without asking us. The most salient was that we wouldn't be able to see my mother. Josie had requisitioned a closed-casket parting.

The next morning, a bleak Monday, thirteen of us are gathered at an enormous hole in ugly Floral Park, New Jersey, to usher my mother to the other world.

Aphra and I and my aunt all want to see my mother one last time before she slides into that hole for good, so we must somehow cajole the surly cemetery boy to open the coffin for us.

"You all gotta come right now," he says, pissed. "I ain't opening the damn thing more than once."

I ask Josie if she wants to come and she sneers lightly, "I've already seen her."

Somehow, she's been buried without makeup, without a change of clothes even, because there is a spatter of red bloodstains on her nightgown. My mother, who never left the house without gorgeous colors on her face, is yellow-brown everywhere I can see, the exact color that my bruises turn.

She has become a thing, much more so than any of the other funeral bodies I've seen: tremendously and unmistakably dead, like a poor large roach found in the kitchen.

She is deader than the frogs and worms I've been given to cut up in school, deader than the deer that I've passed on the road.

Aphra and I have to compete for time with her. I'm afraid the boy is going to shut the lid at any moment, and I want my crack at her. I try to be a good sport when Aphra gets there first. My sister looks like a version of me—gray hair to my dyed blond, short hair, glasses, lesbo profile, regretful expression. We're both cyborgs copied from the prototype my mother found in Kabbalah.

Aphra left home early, but she has hated and loved my

mother all her life, just like me. Now she mutters low to my mother, and touches her. I am crazy with envy, frustration, desire. I know my arms will not be able to reach far enough into the casket to accomplish a touch, not even to fleetingly edge my mother's yellow hand. If only there were someone here I could get to move her arm closer to me, or to lift and push me close enough, right into the coffin.

I don't have a good enough relationship with anyone in the family to ask them to move even part of a dead body for me, or even hoist me a little. Aphra keeps communing with her for what seems like years, decades, eras, finally I actually interject, "May I?"

I am cutting in, at a ballroom: I am the most handsome serviceman in a 40s movie, sure that the lady will prefer me. I am a fake English gentleman enforcing my will with a fake English accent, a phony Oxbridge birthright. (I am the one who speaks the poshest, of my sisters; I'm the one who thrilled the pants off Mom with Yale.) I'm a smiling upper-class, freezing my sister to death at the coffin.

Aphra looks upset and waves her hands around ineffectually, walking away. I pounce on the newly empty space by my mother's side.

I'm glad I get to look at my mother's sweet face, but it's agony that I can't touch her. Her hair, which she has dyed jet black assiduously since I was six, is gray in the coffin, and I feel sorry for her.

In my zeal to tell you about her husk and what we do with it, I have neglected to describe the entire scene for you, reader: On a bare hill, as we wait for the cut-rate, mail-order rabbi, I'm the only one in a colored coat—mustard yellow, almost like my mother's face now. (There was no time to buy a black one.) It was her coat, actually, which she gave to me because I didn't have a good winter coat. So I feel like I am wearing her skin.

I, the golem, walk about on the hill and no one speaks to me. When I arrived I tried to kiss each of my sisters, but Josie just grinned fakely and turned her face away, and Aphra pulled away so hard that my lip just grazed her cheek for a twentieth of a second. An impregnable halo of isolation surrounds each of them. Does one surround me, too? My mother's brother, his wife, my mother's sister and her daughter will not speak to me, either. Are we all islands in this family, or is there something about me in particular that drives all my family away?

I can't believe I have no one here to hug me. Am I leprous, when I need people most? How did I get to this pass?

In the cold wave that emanates from everyone I feel my own inner terribleness confirmed, as though they have discovered I'm the murderer.

CHAPTER 14

When Josie and I were still friends, we had fantasized with so much pleasure about going to the funeral together in a big black limo. On the voluptuous leather seats, we would drink good coffee and eat artisanal chocolates cast in the shape of my mother's face. They were going to be called "little chocolate Mommies." Waiting for her death had consumed so much of our lives that we were determined to mark the occasion with a big bang.

We had loved planning aloud the details together, like girls imagining a coach made out of a pumpkin and mice footmen.

In the end, Josie was upset when I would not travel to the distant cemetery in the limo with her. (I took another car service, one that cost $240 round trip, but at least I could come and go as I pleased.)

I did not feel like commissioning a patissier to make the chocolate Mommies (and as it turned out, there was also no time).

The first two days after my mother was dead, I went to the park to commune with her. There is a stand of old voluptuous cherry trees at Grand Army Plaza, at the very northernmost entrance to Prospect Park, and although it was March and they did not even have their leaves yet, much less their insanely puffed pink flowers like enormous breasts, they were still beautiful with all those wildly lashed-together branches, and I spoke to her there, under the biggest tree.

I was comforted, honey. She could see me from inside that tree, from inside the crazy black branches and roots, and I could see her, and I knew she wished me well.

That day a lovely acquaintance of mine from college, Erin Knightley, baked me a savory cheese pie and delivered it. And though it gave me diarrhea, I really, really appreciated it.

Then three days after the funeral, Josie took it upon herself to mail out a bit of my mother's late writing. There was a letter to Aphra, Josie, and me that my mother had written in the fall, designating which of us should get which of the twenty pieces of jewelry that would still be warm on her corpse at the time of death, as though anticipating that we would be picking over them. And there was an undated bit of her personal writing, not addressed to anyone.

The note assigning the jewelry was full of contrasting personal asides, as though my mother could not contain herself while denominating who got what. To Aphra: "SOMETIMES you need a lot of patience. I have never stopped loving you." To me, next: "I wish you success in all areas of your life, good health, and love." Finally: "Josie, you have been wonderful to me, always here when I needed you, giving me love, support, nurturing. I love you so very much. You made my long sickness bearable. I pray for your health and long life, and wish for you all good things."

Wonderful. My mother had accentuated this unequal list of blessings by giving Josie eleven items of the jewelry that had lately touched her skin, me five and Aphra four.

"I don't want to be a petty, jealous person," my mother wrote in the other letter, the little personal essay. "Which I think I used to be."

Then she said, "How good a mother could I be if two of my children keep away from me? Wouldn't they want to be with me more if doing so would be good for them?" I was one of the two children she meant who kept away from her.

Apparently, visiting once every one or two weeks when she was ill was a sign of my utter repudiation and rejection.

As to why Josie decided to copy and send those letters to Aphra and me immediately after the funeral, you'd have to ask her. Neither of us had called and demanded, "Who gets 'the milky white star-sapphire ring?'" as my mother had described it in her final accounting.

I know I myself have never felt as competitive with my sisters as I did just then, or as ravenously angry at my mother. It was as though she had taken all the love I'd lately felt for her and turned it into hunger, competition, naked need. I felt like Cain and Abel, Joseph and all of his eleven brothers, all of them simultaneously.

Her ghost seemed mysteriously to be getting my sisters and me to scratch and tear at one another for her love even more now than she had while still alive.

In life, she'd certainly directed each of her three golems away from one another as soon as we had stepped off her pottery table. "Josie's very jealous of you, you know." "Aphra's a very sick girl." I don't know what she said to my sisters about me, but she'd always shared with me secrets and lies about them, histories of their sex lives, who had been torn to pieces how and when.

Over and over I would say to her, "I should hear that from her if she wants to tell me about it." For of course, my mother's versions of my sisters' secrets didn't ever draw me closer to them, but always further apart. Then again, she was always telling me my sisters were furious with me (and I'm sure, telling them I was furious with them).

She drove us all away from my father, too, of course—her fourth golem, as it were. One of my sisters remembers our mother discouraging my father from showing us too much affection or picking us up.

Of course, she gave *Qus* points for tormenting him, too. And she had occasionally lavished on my sisters and me the romantic ardor and sweet praise she denied my father. That, reader, I have always supposed to have been the main reason he hit me.

My mother, the trickiest ringmaster, had manipulated us all until the day she died—and even afterwards, we somehow felt, now from beyond the grave.

Early on in their marriage, when my father was still under the control of his own dad, Grandpa Phil, and my mother realized it, my sister remembers her shouting at him, "If anyone's going to control you, I will!" And she did, apparently. From then on.

How do you break a golem spell?

It is not easy, my dear poppet and acolyte.

The only way there is, is feeling pain.

It is not that you need to be given more pain, it is that you need to feel the pain that's there.

There was a lot of pain to go around, for a lot of different reasons. It was my sister Josie, I remembered, who had decided to send the letters at that particular moment, not my mother. Even I myself had caused some of the pain.

In the original Frog Prince story, the Princess does not kiss the frog. Instead, she suddenly throws him hard against the wall, BAM! And when he feels his body break upon the wall the frog turns back into a human man again.

The black knight gets out of C.S. Lewis's Silver Chair by moaning and screaming and foaming at the mouth in physical agony that cannot be counterfeited, asking for help "for the love of God" until his three terrified visitors finally cut him loose from his cords.

It happened in a series of steps, over a long time, reader. It is as though I crashed through a glass wall into a new dimension, the dimension of feeling, where before I had only been in two dimensions like a comic-book character, capable of everything but growth.

My own screaming went on for so long that I could scarcely maintain a hope that it would stop some day.

It hurt. Both before and after she died, for five years.

My arms are what started to hurt, and then my innermost core hurt. Then everything hurt, like an ax inside my chest.

In alchemy, this process is called rotting, burning, and fermenting.

That, reader, is what I did.

I realized that Marla, who wanted me to die, was not a good intern for my needs. So I switched to a man who became my most frequently on-time intern, the sixty-year-old aspiring-gay-journalist John. But he occasionally made hurtful sexist and racist remarks, and sometimes showed up dead drunk.

So. I switched again to a man named Sam from the neighborhood, who I had met because he once had a job delivering laundry to me for the Eco-mat. I had to pay Sam much more than I did my writing interns, but the relationship was clearer. He was never resentful. And, reader, I never felt like I was tricking or cheating him.

He felt compassion for me, I believe, reader, but he was not helping me out of pity. Nor was he helping me because I was offering him sex, or promising to make him a famous writer, or listening to him call me a piece of shit whenever he felt like it.

It was because I was paying him $20 an hour, which felt like an appropriate exchange for his labor.

Sam used to joke in the beginning about what he claimed were "the wild parties" he was sure I was attending, but when I told him the jokes bugged me he never made them again.

And I stopped depending on Eileen to be my only friend, and found a few others who had a little more time to get together because they did not have small children and were not simultaneously embarked on graduate degree programs.

I learned, finally, about the Minkowitz death ray, which had been pulsating from my nervous eyes for all these many years.

Every member of my family employed the Minkowitz death ray, but I had never realized I was using it myself. It was a catalyzed yellow gleam from the eye-stalks, a sort of noxious flare, that turned everyone in the vicinity into a load of foully compressed garbage. There was a nasty smell afterwards for years, like the scent from a Mafia private-carting-company truck. People did not like the ray being used on them, at all. They scarcely wanted to be my friends, after I did.

I had started to observe my own death ray one day, but in the vaguest way I possibly could, out of the corner of my eye. It was when I realized I was using it on the counter people at the fancy coffee bar who hadn't understood where to put my coffee.

I'd felt so frustrated. So helpless and denied. So utterly incapable of getting what I needed.

That ravenous sense of denied need, that frustration and powerlessness that all golems feel, had sparked out of my eyes and made me turn the counterwoman into a mountain of shit.

Though I hadn't understood it at the time, I had actually gotten a very faint *first* glimpse of my foul capacities some eight or nine years previous, with my then-best friend Becka.

It was 1994, and I loved an obnoxious woman named Sara Transom. She had cheated on me and finally broken up with me in a particularly cruel way, insisting that I not tell the acquaintances we were having dinner with that night so she could still bask in my then-fame among lesbians. And she had broken up with me in Minneapolis, where she invited me to come and visit her for a long weekend.

My best friend did not have much time to hear about it when I flew home. I tried calling her that night, but we only got to talk for a minute. Then I tried calling on a couple of mornings. Actually, morning was Becka's designated writing time, I now dimly remember. Reader, I thought my friend was slipping away from me. I thought not only did I not have Sara, I was now under threat of not having Becka, either.

"Hey, Donna," Becka said cheerily, and a bit wearily, when she picked up the phone. "I can't really talk now."

"I wish we could talk more than we do." I tried to point my need out affectionately, jocularly. "Hey, I want more of you than I'm getting!" I said smiling.

To my surprise, she did not take what I said jocularly. "You should wait until I call you back. You know, when you call, I might want to be doing something else. I might want to be writing. Or if I feel like talking on the phone, maybe I'd rather be talking to Dan Lumpson than you." Dan Lumpson was a clown who we had gone to college with, a friend of Becka's.

I was horrified when she said maybe she'd rather be talking to Dan Lumpson than me.

"But we're good friends. What if I really need to talk to you?"

"You have to wait until I call you back. The person who doesn't want to talk, wins!"

I felt so hurt, reader. And so powerless to get what I needed.

I did what I remembered my mother doing in situations like this. Used my internal powers. "No, I'll make you talk to me! You'll talk to me whether you want to or not."

Becka did not like the death ray and she never spoke to me again.

I don't know if I ever used it again on other actual friends after that. It was Olive who first told me about my weapon, six years later, because I'd used it on *her*.

How did she describe the infernal thing? I can barely remember a word of it now. Perhaps she just said I became very hard to take sometimes when I was angry.

Part of the spell that governs use of the death ray

involves a deep forgetting while the golem is making use of it, as though the golem had been moving in a dream. But the murder-ray is woven into us, just as deeply as the white thread that is only there so our masters can cut it to erase *Qus*.

"I've never seen what you're talking about," I said to my shrink stiffly. "However, I'm willing to believe I might be doing it, because you've said other things that turned out to be true."

After that, I actually observed myself using the weapon a few times, with strangers. I understood what I was doing to the coffee counterwoman, at the very moment I was turning her into a pile of dung. I understood what I was doing a year later, when a group of twenty insufferable radical drummers decided to perform on the street in front of my window for half an hour.

I went downstairs and made them stop, by touching them and sucking the life force out of them.

They weren't an imminent threat to my life, although they felt like it. Part of me cracked that day. I was no longer able to assume that I was innocent, and powerless. And survival stopped being the thing I wanted at all costs.

In the *rubedo* (fermenting) phase, right after a final shattering of contaminants there is something called "the peacock's tail" in the substance that is being worked on, a brilliant display of colors that resembles the colors of spring after winter, or the Aurora Borealis in the sky.

I started hanging out with storytellers, people who don't even believe in writing the damn thing down. And I started going to a gaggle of dating events—yes, dating events, little reader. In New York, it can be hard to meet people, especially if you're a lesbian.

I'd always had a most laborious, awkward, and terrified time flirting. Because I was so frightened of every person I was attracted to.

Lots of them looked like my mother. The femmes, in

particular, were inviting and sparkly in the same way she had been. I felt as though every time I wanted a woman, I was contaminating her with my disgusting desire. I felt I was doing something horrible to her. Part of the golem-magic that had bound me to my mother was the trap she'd laid for me of frustration and desire, of seduction and humiliation, and it had bound me in my interactions with all other women, too, for all these years.

"If anyone's going to control you, I will!"

But Pilates, which I had begun studying at a place called the Integrative Care Center, taught that I could "integrate" all my many parts—including the part that wanted to kiss and go on dates—and develop a practice of wholeness, of entirety, through which I would not be able to be controlled by anyone but me.

I'm not kidding you. It was Pilates! Mr. Joseph Pilates had developed it in an internment camp for German citizens in England during World War I, where he himself was a prisoner. He called it a "return to life," and it was a way that physically weak, wounded, and exhausted persons, locked up for their nationality alone, could, by trying and receiving help, become strong even if they'd never been so before.

In "contrololgy," as Joseph originally called his method, all the various muscles of the body were supposed to be "cooperative and loyal" to one another, each supporting the others so that no one body part (the lower back, say, or the knee) had an unhealthy burden. All aspects of one's body, mind, and spirit were supposed to work mutually. No part was the slave, as it were, and no part was the exploitive master, lording it over the others. Being "loyal" to one another—integrated—they would develop—finally—a happy living structure in which each cell contributed to let the whole move around "with minimum effort and maximum pleasure."

I was surprised by how my teacher, Red, was able to help me develop strength in my stomach and legs that helped uncurl my twisted torso and draw life into my shoulders and arms and hands.

After two months, I was able to bend in ways I hadn't been able to in twenty years. I hadn't imagined I would ever be able to do leg-raises again—after a back injury I had gotten from my crappy student job in the Yale library. Then, after my arms were blighted, I did not think I would ever be able to curl my chest open. Or get enough circulation into my shoulders again that I would actually be able to build muscles in that place. Before I started training with Red, the return of what Joseph called the "pure, fresh blood" into my shoulders had been too painful to tolerate.

Pilates was a method of integration, not of magic. As Dr. Mayhew advised, I kept using voice dictation software, because typing could easily reinjure me. I continued not carrying groceries, or bags of trash, and let my arms get stronger gradually. As Red suggested, I allowed Dr. Sing's mantra to apply for me also to Pilates: "Little by little, step by step."

And in fact, I was enjoying life so much more this way. I felt *feelings* from the tips of my toes to the top of my head. My head felt effervescent, as though a flowery beer had been poured into it and my hair was curling up from the blood vessels in my scalp to the tips of my curls. The response I got at the dating events was, startlingly, strengthening my ego as much as Pilates was strengthening my spine. I found that women were attracted to me.

Learning that I was attractive was rather shocking. But nice. It made flirting ever so much pleasanter. Olive got me started by dinning into me that if, by chance, I ever asked out someone who said no, that did not make me shameful and disgusting.

She said, "People get rejected *most of the time* when they ask someone out. There's no shame to it whatsoever."

In 2003, I met—at an event called Date Bait—a pretty young woman named Dulcie. She was sweeter and more loving than anyone I had been with previously, and also, I believe, prettier.

Like I told you, good-looking women had terrified me, reader!

I dated her for seven months, but honey, she turned out to be much nastier than *me* when she got mad, made jokes about my being Jewish, and was "afraid of my vagina" as she told me, which explained why she didn't want to touch it very much at all.

We broke up. Olive said, "What a great chance this was to practice!"

But when I was still seeing Dulcie, both my dead parents had begun coming to me to tell me they were sorry, often in public bathrooms. They particularly liked the bathrooms of the Cosi Sandwich Bar, which were always colorful, bright orange, and clean. But they also liked Dulcie's bathroom in Bronxville, and enjoyed visiting me out in the open, among the chairs and tables, at Starbucks.

My father had come to me now and again in a low-key fashion, and smiled, or sometimes cried, over the years. But now he was a just bit more physically present than he'd been, and now my mother was suddenly coming, too, and she would say silently to me, telepathically as it seemed, "I'm sorry I hurt you" and "I wish you well." I could see her face as she said it, at the same time sad, regretful, and loving. Her face had lost some of its prednisone puffiness. She and my father had both been utterly healed, they told me, and loved me very much from wherever they were.

I spent even more time with the storytellers, who were part of a strange new movement to put new life into the oral tradition of myth and fairy tales.

A few of them were shamans, but none were wizards as far as I could tell. These wandering folks were into sharing power with others, not accruing it. I went to even more dating events then, and as I experienced the happiness of casually talking to women it felt like spring after winter, and sun on the leaves. I went to the Sundance Outdoor Adventure Society, and Women About, voluntary organizations that went on hikes up mountains and had spaghetti dinners, respectively. I went to the Girls Meet Girls at Brighton Beach bathing party and Russian-food jaunt, where I made a date with a woman who seemed full of life and turned out to be a member of the New Alliance Party, a neofascist cult. But I was amused and only a little ticked off when I found out.

I went to Date Bait several times, where I always met women I liked. I went to a venture called Deeper Dating, which was not light enough for me by half and included a therapist warning us at the get-go that it was extraordinarily difficult and painful to enter new relationships. I even went to Congregation Beth Simchat Torah's Lesbian and Gay Speed Dating event, where I, a former golem, exchanged numbers with a young Orthodox Jewish medical student and a semi-trans looker with a bow tie.

Eventually, I made my way back to Date Bait, my perennial best event. I knew the ropes by now, and so I understood that I was not limited to meeting the women by filling out the little SAT-like computer form with pencil in the right circles, and officially "matching" with them in the Date Bait owner Rafael's proprietary computer program. You "matched" if you put someone's identifying Date Bait number on your scorecard and if they also put your Date Bait number on theirs.

When the July 2005 Date Bait was over, I had matched with six women, but the one I really wanted to talk to had been busy during the entire official "chat each other up" segment. A flock of girls had been monopolizing her in turn. In the seventy-person microphone go-round that every Date Bait begins with, this woman said she was interested in finding someone "passionate and intellectual." I figured I could probably fit in that description. But more than that, she just seemed extraordinarily *pleasant*, reader.

"Cute," I wrote in my notes. But beyond that, there was a mysterious *welcoming quality* to her, as though she had the scents of lavender and lemon verbena on her fingers and iris root emanating from her chest.

In Pilates, "teachers start with sense organs," as Joseph says in his book. "We must...really be able to enjoy ourselves... All forms of play tend materially to renew our vitality... The term 'play' as we use it here, embraces every possible form of PLEASURABLE LIVING."

I had never known an unthreatening sense of play before, certainly not from my lovers. Yet it seemed to emanate from this woman. Most peculiarly, there was a singing tenderness coming out of her breastbone, like the warmth from a camp stove.

I knew I wasn't going to match with this woman because we hadn't spoken. But I decided to go up to her at the very end.

"Hi," I said. "I didn't get a chance to talk to you, but I really wanted to."

Karen smiled at me. "Keep talking to me. Just walk around with me, though, because I need to sweep." She had gotten free admission by working the event for nothing, and Rafael was a hard taskmaster, insisting that she not only sign women in during the first hour and collect their computer cards during the second, but sweep the floor when the shindig was over.

When I saw her later that week at our first real date, I got a better look at her. She was a femme, but much taller than my mother, like a beautiful drag queen. We were eating ham and cheese sandwiches with loud-tasting pickles at a wine bar. Our knees knocked together under the table.

On a stoop a block away, where she kissed me, everything felt simultaneously goofy, perfumed, and alluring. Homeless men panhandling at the subway entrance laughed at us for kissing. She put my hands on her ass. Nobody had ever done *that* before! I thought she looked exactly like the ancient Greek goddess called the Lady of Wild Things, and in fact I soon discovered she could make plants grow practically by breathing on them. She did silly voices of frogs and ducks to entertain me: "Quack. Quack. Quack. *Ribbit!*" After we'd spent a few months together, I found out she'd been kidnapped and raised by a goblin family in the Mines of Moria, but had escaped. She danced her way out, because the sight of dancing, I have learned, makes goblins lose their screws. We moved into a convenient apartment in a leafy, ungentrified neighborhood. Sometimes all you need to recover your lost kingdom is good access to the R train. Reader, I married her.

EPILOGUE

Recently, I came home to her one evening after physical therapy. "What's a good definition for gender?" Karen asked idly. She was preparing to give a sociology midterm, and ironing both of our shirts at the same time. I kissed her mouth, which always tasted like a particularly vivid and purple sort of plum, and began to chop up an onion for our tomato meat sauce. I got the pasta out ("The squiggly ones!" Karen cried happily, "my favorite!"), and was delighted with how the chopped tomatoes glowed as they sizzled in the pan. I looked over the draft of Karen's equally sizzling, radical midterm, while she began reading my day's pages. As I lit candles, Karen kissed my face. "I don't know how I got here," I shouted, "but I'm never going back."

ACKNOWLEDGMENTS

Many people helped me with this book. Eileen Kelly and Ann Darby nourished this idea from a small spark, and gave me vital suggestions. Matt Mitler, Vincent Collazo, and Karen Lippitt read a gazillion drafts and gave me feedback, and Jane Shufer and Mishti Roy provided crucial advice at critical junctures. Karen Schechner gave me the sort of magical aid that helpful animals do in fairy tales, and Vicki Nevins made sure I was on the right page with my depictions of RSI. Elyaqim Mosheh Adam generously looked over the Hebrew and Yiddish (though any errors are my own), and Vincent Collazo kindly converted the entire manuscript to Word for me. I really don't think they make literary agents as sterling as Valerie Borchardt anymore. Nor do they make dream publishers like Don Weiseat Magnus Books.

A half dozen or so dedicated and imaginative health professionals have helped me to heal (to one extent or another) from RSI. I cannot say how grateful I am to Aija Paegle, PT, Steven Fetherhuff, CPI, Dr. Susan Richman, Dr. Ming Liu, Dr. Ming Zeng, and Dr. D.S.V., and to a succession of massage therapists including the nurturing and smart Vlada Yaneva, LMT.

There just aren't any words to thank Karen Lippitt for cohabiting with me.

ABOUT THE AUTHOR

Donna Minkowitz's first book, *Ferocious Romance: What My Encounters with the Right Taught Me about Sex, God and Fury*, won a Lambda Literary Award. It was also shortlisted for the Quality Paperback Book Club's New Visions Award "for the most promising and distinctive work by a new writer." She was a columnist on LGBT politics and culture for the *Village Voice* from 1987 to 1995, as well as a political columnist for *The Advocate*. She has also written for the *New York Times Book Review*, *New York magazine*, *Salon*, and *The Nation*. Minkowitz won the Exceptional Merit Media Award for "In the Name of the Father," a creative nonfiction piece in which she disguised herself as a sixteen-year-old Christian evangelical boy to write about the Promise Keepers for Ms. She has appeared on *Charlie Rose* and many NPR programs. She lives in New York.